I Think, Therefore I Have a Headache!

Books by Martha Bolton

FROM BETHANY HOUSE PUBLISHERS

Didn't My Skin Used to Fit?

I Think, Therefore I Have a Headache!

MARTHA BOLTON

I Think, Therefore I Have a Headache!

A Laugh-Out-Loud Look at Life

BETHANYHOUSE
MINNEAPOLIS, MN 55438

Published by Bethany House Publishers
11400 Hampshire Avenue South
Bloomington, Minnesota 55438
www.bethanyhouse.com

Bethany House Publishers is a Division of
Baker Book House Company, Grand Rapids, Michigan.

Printed in the United States of America

Library of Congress Cataloging-in-Publication Data

Bolton, Martha, 1951-
    I think, therefore I have a headache! : a laugh-out-loud look at life by Martha Bolton.
      p. cm.
    ISBN 0-7642-2625-8 (pbk.)
    1. American wit and humor.   I. Title.
    PN6165.B65   2003
    814'.54—dc21   2003001451

In memory of Barney McNulty,
creator of the cue cards.
No one held our jokes better than he.

MARTHA BOLTON is a full-time comedy writer and the author of over fifty books. She has been a staff writer for Bob Hope for fifteen years along with writing for Mark Lowry, Jeff Allen, Ann Jillian, Phyllis Diller, and many others. Her material has appeared in *Reader's Digest, Chicken Soup for the Soul* books, and *Brio* magazine, and she has received four Angel awards and both an Emmy nomination and a Dove Award nomination. Martha and her husband live in Tennessee.

Acknowledgments

To my husband, Russ, for always being the balance in my life.

To my family, for so many great memories.

To Steve Laube, my editor and friend. Thank you for giving me a reason to stay out of the kitchen.

And finally to all of you who have ever suffered a "life" headache, thank you for picking up this book. Think of it as literary aspirin. But don't just read two chapters and call me in the morning. Read it all. In fact, read all the humor books you can get your hands on. Watch comedies. Watch cartoons. Watch politicians. You don't have to worry about exceeding eight doses of laughter a day. You can have as much as you want. It's calorie free. Enjoy!

Few minds wear out; more rust out.

Christian Nestell Bovee

Contents

I Think, Therefore I Have a Headache

*It was such a lovely day I
thought it a pity to get up.*

W. SOMERSET MAUGHAM

They say Socrates once stood in a single spot all day and night pondering some deep philosophical issue. This man was thought to be a genius.

If he were alive today and did that, he would be thought to be in the way.

"Move it, Soc," his wife would say. *"Why do you always gotta stand right where I'm trying to vacuum?"*

Most of us in today's society don't have the patience for profound thinkers. We don't care how deeply someone is contemplating the meaning of life, if he or she is taking one millisecond too long to move their foot from the brake pedal to the gas pedal after the traffic light has turned green, we're gonna start honking. It's not that we don't want people to think, we just don't want them holding up the flow of traffic to do it.

Is it any wonder, then, that deep philosophical thinkers seem to be on the endangered species list? We're in far too much of a hurry to put up with them, much less appreciate them. We don't want people slowing down our pace while they ponder the big questions of the universe. We don't want them in line in front of us at the bank, we don't want them blocking the grocery store aisles, and for heaven's sake, they'd better not even think about holding up the line at the all-you-can-eat buffet! (Is there anything worse than getting stuck behind someone whose mind has drifted off to places unknown while you're trying to reach for the fried chicken?)

Maybe we're jealous. Most of us don't have—or at least we don't allow ourselves—time to think, so we resent it when others seem to do it so guiltlessly. We would love to have the luxury of pondering the mysteries of life, but our day planners are way too full. How do you schedule time for deep thought when you're still trying to squeeze in time to breathe? Who among us would ever jot down an entry like "Wednesday, 3–4 P.M.: Ponder"? It would never happen. We need to be here at 3:15, there at 3:30, and somewhere else at 3:45. Allot a portion of our precious time to just sit and think? You've got to be kidding!

I'm afraid Socrates never would have survived today's crowded schedules. There are too many meetings to go to, projects to work on, e-mails that need answering, and kids who need to be picked up from soccer practice, piano lessons, karate classes, and gymnastics. We're too busy living life to take any time to actually contemplate it.

Even the arts are affected by this full-throttle speed of ours. If Auguste Rodin were commissioned to create his famous sculpture *The Thinker* today, he probably couldn't do it. No one would sit still long enough to pose for it. And even if someone did, the cell phone in his hand and that Palm Pilot strapped to his waist would give the statue a whole different look anyway.

More of us need to be like Socrates and just stop in the middle of the room and ponder to our heart's content. Our world desperately needs more thinkers. We need people who aren't afraid to take the time to figure out the whos, whats, whens, wheres, and whys of life. Socrates may not have made many friends blocking the buffet lines of his day, but because he allowed himself the time and space to think, he was able to come up with some pretty interesting thoughts that otherwise might have been lost. Thoughts that we're still passing around in our e-mails today.

But profound thinking doesn't thrive in the middle of rush hour traffic or a crowded mall. It takes slowing down, listening to your heart, and being open to learning something new about yourself and the world we live in. And maybe even having a good laugh about it all.

That's what this book is about—thinking. And laughing. Thinking about how much our world has changed over the years. And how much it has stayed the same. Thinking about both the tragedies and the comedies of life. Thinking about politics, faith, family, health food, exercise, air travel, modern conveniences, and more.

Thinking—it's not for the lazy or the uncommitted. Years ago Rodin said of his famous sculpture, ". . . he thinks not only with his brain, with his knitted brow, his distended nostrils and compressed lips, but with every muscle of his arms, back and legs, with his clenched fist and gripping toes."

Auguste knew that if it's done right, thinking is a full-body exercise. That's why Socrates stopped everything else to do it.

Thinking is hard work. No wonder it can really give us a headache!

> *Any idiot can face a crisis—it's*
> *this day-to-day living that wears*
> *you out.*
> ANTON CHEKHOV

2

Just a Spoonful of Sugar Helps the Trilipathorphan Go Down

It's no longer a question of staying healthy. It's a question of finding a sickness you like.

JACKIE MASON

Speaking of headaches, have you seen those commercials for all the new miracle drugs that have recently come onto the market? The goal of these ads is to pique our interest enough so that we'll ask our doctor to prescribe the new medicines for us. But after watching a few of the commercials, asking for these medications might be the last thing we'd want to do.

"TRILIPATHORPHAN* is not for everybody," the voiceover

*Any resemblance to a real drug is purely coincidental.

announcer begins. *"In some instances it has been known to cause disorientation, loss of muscle control, full body rash, spontaneous uncontrollable bleeding, and a profound desire to sing old Broadway tunes. Ask your doctor if Trilipathorphan is right for you."*

I have a feeling there must be some sort of legal requirement to recite the side effects of medications like this because I can't imagine a pharmaceutical company adding these warnings to their commercials voluntarily. They do their best to downplay these side effects, however, by simultaneously showing visuals of flowers, puppies, waterfalls, babbling brooks, grassy fields, and other soothing scenes. So while television viewers are watching puppies play and a delicate little sparrow drink out of a peaceful creek, the announcer states soothingly that in a few isolated cases patients using the new drug have had their liver explode. The puppies continue to frolic and the little birdie drinks on. A couple of seagulls fly overhead, a wave splashes ever so gently over some rocks, and the drug is pitched one last time: *"Trilipathorphan—it only shuts down minor organs."*

I suppose most thinking adults would agree, though, that being told precisely what the side effects of any medication could be, no matter how scary, is a good thing. So if Trilipathorphan sounds right for you, go ahead and talk to your doctor about it. After all, like their slogan says, *"Trilipathorphan—if it doesn't kill you, it just might help."*

> *If you live to be one hundred, you've got it made. Very few people die past that age.*
> GEORGE BURNS

3

I Can't Believe It's Food

I don't even butter my bread. I consider that cooking.

KATHERINE CEBRIAN

I've made a living joking about my bad cooking. Unfortunately for my dinner guests, the stories are true. Once I actually incinerated a turkey in my oven. (It was a smoked turkey and I didn't know that smoked meant it was already cooked. Some seventeen hours later I had a pan full of turkey jerky.)

I've made Bundt cakes that were more like lava rocks, biscuits that made the dining table sag, and I've had soufflés implode in my oven on too many occasions to list in a book of this size.

Still, even with all my culinary disasters, my cooking has never made the evening news, nor have my dinner guests had to spend the night in the hospital. (They were treated in the emergency room but never admitted.)

Yet how many times have you heard about some fast-food restaurant sending dozens of customers to the hospital doubled over in pain? "Ten people got sick." "Twenty people." "Fifty." The reports aren't commonplace, but they certainly have happened.

Now, granted, anyone can make a mistake. A worker forgets to wipe the countertop where he just sliced up the chicken parts or handled the meat patties, and the next thing you know it's "Botulism burgers for everyone!"

Or maybe the cook didn't fry or broil the meat long enough to kill all the bacteria.

Or maybe what customers thought was beef wasn't. Maybe it was kangaroo instead.

But even that we forgive. Why? Because we love eating out. We're addicted to fast food. We're not like our ancestors, who had to hunt the animal first, then sweat all day over a hot fire preparing the meal for the family.

"How's the bison, hon?"

"Delicious!"

"It's too salty, isn't it? I knew it was going to be too salty."

Times have changed. There aren't a lot of us roasting bison over an open fire these days. Today, we sweat for fifteen minutes in a drive-thru lane and think we've cooked.

"You won't believe what I just went through! There were eight cars in front of me! I'm exhausted!"

Because we love eating out, our response to a fast-food chain that has been cited with food poisoning is amazingly forgiving.

"Twelve cases of food poisoning? That was a year ago. I'm sure they've wiped down the counter by now."

"Kangaroo meat? Big deal. I've had pocket sandwiches before."

If it's our favorite restaurant, health violations or not, we gladly turn the other fork.

But let's be honest, shall we? Would we be this forgiving with anyone else's cooking? If Grandma Blanchard's Salmonella Au Gratin had everyone doubling over and being rushed off to the hospital after the Fourth of July church potluck, I don't think too many of us would line up to taste test the delicacy the following year, do you?

"I'd stay away from the potatoes if I were you," we'd whisper to the visitors as they moved along in the serving line. *"I know you're new, but you're just going to have to trust us on this one."*

And wouldn't you like to know who's in charge of the packaging and marketing of some of the food products on the grocery store shelves today? I was in our local supermarket last week and made an interesting discovery in the dairy case. Not only did they have I Can't Believe It's Not Butter in both tubs and cubes, now they've added a new Is It Butter? brand of margarine. It makes you wonder what's next: Very Nearly Butter; Could Be Butter; Looks Like Butter to Me; or If It's Not Butter, What in the World Is It?

And there's another company that's now offering catsup in different colors. If you close your eyes (which is how my family eats most of my cooking anyway), it tastes just like regular catsup. Only instead of being red, it's green! Bright green. Or purple. It also comes in a new "mystery color" bottle that doesn't let you know what color you're going to get until you squeeze it out.

Margarine manufacturers have also stepped up to the color palette with the introduction of a squeeze bottle that dispenses blue margarine. That's right, blue. We can now squeeze blue margarine onto our pancakes, waffles, and biscuits. It's like eating breakfast at Papa Smurf's. I don't know what the fat content is, but if it ever clogs up our arteries, it'll give a whole new definition to blue blood.

And have you ever wondered who it is that names all the new breakfast cereals? Lately, it seems like the movie and cartoon industries have been having a little too much influence in this area. We've had Spiderman cereal, Power Puff Girls cereal, and Batman cereal, and that's just to name a few.

But what if cereal companies go overboard and start using other movies or movie stars for their marketing? We could end up with cereals like Children of the Corn Flakes, Apple Jack Nicholson, and Shredded Wheat and Enron Documents.

The last word on food, though, has to be Spam. Think about it—where would any of us be without that little can of ham wannabe? I, for one, grew up on Spam. I know it gets ridiculed a lot, but to be perfectly honest, I actually like it. It's never too tough (you can cut it with a spoon), it's already cooked so I don't have to worry about overcooking it, and I'm pretty sure it has some sort of nutritional value. As a matter of fact, I like it so much, I'm thinking about shaping it into the form of a turkey and serving it next Thanksgiving.

Keep that under your hat, though. I'd hate for Emeril to beat me to it.

> *Old people shouldn't eat health foods. They need all the preservatives they can get.*
> ROBERT ORBEN

4

Just Don't Do It

*Even a mosquito doesn't get a
slap on the back until
it starts to work.*

ANONYMOUS

We're too pampered, and as a result, we've become lazy. If you don't believe me, think about the last time you sat through a television program you didn't want to watch just because the remote was on the other side of the room, or when you used your cell phone to page your daughter upstairs to tell her to come down and eat dinner.

We hardly have to do anything for ourselves anymore.

Thanks to all the computer games on the market today, we can hunt, fish, golf, wrestle, skateboard, surf, play football, baseball, or basketball, or do just about any other sport we want without ever leaving the house. Some of us wouldn't even sweat at all if it weren't for our skin sticking to our vinyl recliners.

We don't even have to fill out our own checks anymore. At some stores, all we have to do is sign our name and the rest of the information is filled in at the register by the computer.

There are voice-activated programs for our personal computers that will transcribe whatever we say into written text. All we have to do is start talking and our words magically appear on the screen as we speak. It's a great idea, especially for people with carpal tunnel syndrome, but you have to be careful what you say to yourself while writing that e-mail to your boss. Your PC could end up typing all the grumbling that you're doing under your breath and you could be standing in an unemployment line faster than you can say, "You've got mail!"

There are voice-activated VCRs and DVDs now, too. All we have to do is speak a command and they'll obey.

"Record Channel 4, Tuesday 8 P.M."

"Rewind."

"Fast-forward."

"Make a bowl of popcorn."

"Do the laundry."

Our wish is their command.

Speaking of laundry, housework has gotten easier, too. We have microwaves that will do the cooking for us in a fraction of the time, self-cleaning ovens that will clean up after us, and I just read where there's a new machine that'll even fold our clothes!

We don't have to do our own exercising anymore, either. All we have to do is buy a special belt that will send an electrical charge to our muscles, "tricking" them into thinking we're exercising. That's right, now we can get six-pack abs while we nap. No work. No sweat. No effort at all, except of course for the energy expelled writing out that check for $39.99.

Frankly, I don't think I'd like an electrical charge playing mind games with my muscles. My muscles and I have built up a certain amount of trust over the years. We have an understanding. I don't make them do anything they don't want to do, and they don't complain about all the cellulite crowding in on their turf. But now, if I start electrocuting them for no good reason, who knows how they might react? That's why I still prefer to exercise the old-fashioned way—aerobics videos. There's nothing quite like the endorphin rush I get from exercise videos. Push the tape into the VCR, eject it, push it in, eject it, and a one and a two . . .

I'm getting winded right now just thinking about it.

We don't have to exert ourselves in the car anymore, either. Many car designs now have the seat belt automatically fastening around us as soon as we shut the door. Apparently, reaching over our shoulder, grabbing the belt, and fastening the metal clasps ourselves was causing too many back injuries.

We also don't have to strain our muscles trying to open and close road maps. A computer system can be installed in our cars that will tell us exactly where we are and in what direction we need to go to get where we need to be. It tells us to turn right, turn left, and if asked, will flawlessly direct us to the nearest outlet shopping mall.

Some airports even provide us with sidewalks that move. Having grown up in the Los Angeles area and survived multiple earthquakes, moving sidewalks aren't that new of a concept for me. But for all those cities where moving sidewalks are a novelty, these do seem to be a popular way to help passengers get to their proper gates.

And have you been to a public rest room lately? We don't have to turn on our own faucets anymore. All we have to do is wave our hands under the spout and the water will automatically gush out (or at least trickle out) and we didn't have to do an ounce of work for it. When we're done, we simply move our hands away and the faucet will shut off all by itself. Eventually.

The faucet isn't the only thing that's gone automatic in public rest rooms. Some rest rooms are so accommodating, we don't even have to press the handle on the . . . well, you know.

We just stand up and walk out and everything takes care of itself automatically. No handle to push, no pedal to step on. It can be a little unsettling, though, when new water starts gushing in well before you're expecting it.

Yes, as a people we are spoiled. We look for dinners that take two minutes to cook in our microwave instead of five, and we audibly sigh if the directions on the box require us to stir at the halfway point.

Aw, I gotta stir? See what else is in the freezer.

Even reading has gotten easier. Thanks to audiobooks, we can read novels and how-to books while we drive, which is great. Unless, of course, it's a boring book; then listening and driving could be hazardous, especially if we fall asleep at the wheel.

"You been drinking?"

"No, officer. Just reading."

"Audiobooks?"

"How'd you know?"

"The open CD case there on the passenger seat. So how many have you had?"

"This is my third."

"Okay . . . outta the car! I'm taking you in!"

Audiobooks—they're a great idea, but know your limit.

Thanks to speakerphones, we don't have to waste any energy holding our telephone, either. All we have to do is talk into the air and the other party hears us crystal clear. Of course, they can also hear our kids wrestling in the background and our dog whining about having to eat leftovers again.

We're so pampered our alarm clocks are even afraid to wake us up. Instead, they timidly coax our eyes open. *"I don't mean to bother you,"* the clock apologizes from out of the darkness, *"but it's time to get up now. You don't feel like it? All right, I'll give you another ten minutes."*

Let's face it, snooze alarms are the wimps of the time-telling industry.

There are plenty more examples that can be cited to prove we're pampered, but I believe the point has been made. And I'm not at all sure that this pampering has been good for us.

When the Y2K scare was running rampant, some people were taking to the mountains, buying houses in the woods with wells and generators, and reading books on how to can fruits and vegetables. People who didn't even eat fruits and vegetables somehow thought they'd want to if the world was suddenly coming to an end. But think about it—had the Y2K problem really happened and society was forced to revert back to the days of yore, how many of us would have even made it to the end of the week?

Maybe it's time we quit allowing ourselves all this pampering and start doing a few more things for ourselves, if only to build up our survival muscles. After all, how could we ever live off the land when all we're used to is living in a drive-thru lane? If a true world-wide emergency were to take place, would we really be able to cope? Think about it—no TVs, no microwaves, no ATMs. Could we survive? I'm afraid many of us wouldn't. That's why we need to start doing more things for ourselves now. We need to go back to the basics and build up those pioneer instincts. We need to . . .

On second thought, maybe I'll just hit the snooze button again and think about all this later.

> **Anyone can do any amount of work provided it isn't the work he is supposed be doing at that moment.**
> ROBERT BENCHLEY

5

Space Wars

Politics ain't worrying this country one-tenth as much as where to find a parking space.

WILL ROGERS

We're losing our space. Have you noticed? I'm not talking about the "go where no man has gone before" kind of space. I'm talking about the "You have yours, I have mine, so let's stay out of each other's and all will be right with the world" kind of space.

Just about everywhere we go now, there's a crowd, or at least it seems that way. It's not like the good ol' days. Back then, if you sat down on a park bench and someone sat down at the opposite end, that empty space in the middle was still considered your space. No one else would even think about sitting in it. Those were the boundaries and no one dared to cross them.

But the world has gotten unbelievably crowded now, and our space is continually being invaded. It's almost impossible to have any privacy or solitude anymore. We go to the mall, it's packed. We go to our favorite restaurant, there's a two-hour wait. We go to an amusement park, the lines go on forever. We go to church and we have to drive to another zip code to find a place to park. Don't get me wrong. Most congregations love visitors. They just wish they'd carpool. Those parking spaces are for the regular attenders. (Yes, it's true that Deacon Williams always takes up two parking spaces when he parks, and no one has parked in the Volunteer of the Week parking space for twelve years, but they figure that still doesn't mean they should surrender their space.)

In places like New York, it's not uncommon for the maître d' of a restaurant to seat two couples who haven't seen each other before in their lives at the same table in order to accommodate the crowds. If it's ever happened to you, you know these can be very awkward situations. You do your best to put up an invisible divider and try to avoid eye contact with the strangers, but that's difficult when they're using your salad fork.

Nowhere is your space more violated than in hotel bathtubs. Who do they build these little "tubettes" for, anyway? Some hotel bathtubs are so small, the only way you can fit in them is to hang your legs off the side and take your bath one body part at a time.

Airlines, too, are notorious for crowding us. First they squeeze us into the waiting areas, then they squeeze us through the gate, then they tell us to squeeze our carry-on luggage into the overhead compartments, and finally they squeeze us into our seats.

I remember one particular flight where I got stuck with a center seat. I always ask for an aisle seat because I'm tall, but the clerk at the ticket counter said the plane was full and I'd have to keep my center seat.

I wasn't happy, but there wasn't anything I could do. So I boarded the plane and sat down in my seat.

As the rest of the passengers filed by, I prayed that the seats on either side of me would remain empty. I even thought about praying and fasting, which wouldn't have been that much of a sacrifice considering most airline food.

I looked up from my prayer and immediately noticed a neck moving down the aisle toward me. At first that's all I saw. Just a neck. A very large neck. Slowly, the rest of him began to come into focus, as did the lady and her equally ample neck who was following closely behind him. It was obvious that the couple heading toward me were professional wrestlers.

No, I thought to myself. *Please, God, no.*

But sometimes God answers yes.

They stopped at my row. The woman indicated that she had the window seat, but before I could stand up to let her in, she climbed over me (not unlike a scissor hold) and took her seat. The guy sat in the aisle seat. There I was, sandwiched between these two supersized human beings for the next three hours. I did not need a blanket. What I needed was my space. Of course, I didn't tell them that. I just smiled and waited until we landed to resume breathing.

Even our cemeteries are losing space. Some of them are so crowded, they're burying the dearly departed right on top of each other. Maybe that's how some people want to be buried, but I think I'd prefer my gravesite to be a one-story.

As the world gets more and more populated, we're going to continue losing our personal space. We can either surrender or we can do our best to hold the line against the intrusion. It's up to us. Personally, I lean toward holding the line. We need to protect our secluded areas where we can rest, relax, and think. It doesn't matter if it's a park, the beach, or just in our own backyards; we can't allow the world to crowd in on these personal hideaways where we find our peace and solitude. And our space.

Life's too important to be crowded out.

I would rather sit on a pumpkin,
and have it all to myself, than be
crowded on a velvet cushion.

HENRY DAVID THOREAU

6

What's in a Name?

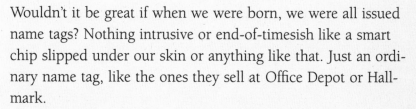

*One survey found that 10 percent
of Americans thought Joan of
Arc was Noah's wife.*

ROBERT BOYNTON

Wouldn't it be great if when we were born, we were all issued name tags? Nothing intrusive or end-of-timesish like a smart chip slipped under our skin or anything like that. Just an ordinary name tag, like the ones they sell at Office Depot or Hallmark.

Think about it—never again would we find ourselves in one of those awkward situations where we've run into someone we recognize but can't for the life of us remember their name.

"Wait a minute . . . wait a minute . . . it's coming to me . . . I know that face . . . that voice . . . just give me a little more time . . . Mom!"

As a society, we already know the advantage that a name tag gives us at office parties, business conventions, and church gatherings. Even though we grumble to ourselves when we're asked to fill out a name tag, down deep we know we'd be lost without it.

Name tags also come in handy (and should be mandatory

and written in large print) at high-school reunions. Maybe not so much at the ten-year reunion, but certainly at every one after that. People change. That cheerleader who had those perfect pearly white teeth may look completely different now that they're removable. And that good-looking football player might be a little harder to recognize now that his once muscular chest has proceeded to regions southward.

I'd even be happy if a name tag just had the person's first name written on it. After all, first names are all they had to work with in Bible times, and they seemed to manage the introductions all right.

"Moses, meet Joshua. Joshua, Moses." Simple and direct. Nothing complicated. And even if they were ever really stumped, all they'd have to do is go through a few genealogies and before long the name of the stranger would come to them.

"Say, aren't you Sadoc, son of Azor, son of Eliakim, son of Abiud?"

"No. That's my cousin."

There are, of course, times when you might not want to be wearing a name tag. Like when the clerk has to tell you that you're over your limit on your Macy's credit card and your transaction has been declined. At times like that, it's probably not a good idea to turn around and let the people standing in line behind you read *Rev. Harold P. Neely* on your lapel. (But then again, they might put a little more in the offering the following Sunday.)

John Donne, a famous thinker, once said, "No man is an island." And he was right. We need friends. Name tags help us to expand our "friend pool."

Name tags are a friend magnet, a welcome mat, an ice-breaker. They're our invitation to come into someone's world and get to know them a little better and for them to get to know us. And in a world where so many of us are strangers, that's a good thing.

A friend may well be reckoned
the masterpiece of Nature.

RALPH WALDO EMERSON

7
Brain Workouts

I have flabby thighs, but
fortunately my stomach
covers them.

JOAN RIVERS

Exercise is supposed to be good for the mind. If that's true, then brain exercises must really be healthy. No, I'm not talking about solving brainteasers, doing crossword puzzles, taking IQ tests, or anything like that. I'm talking about exercises *in* the brain. In other words, doing push-ups and sit-ups, jogging, cross-country skiing, weight lifting, even Iditarod racing, but doing it all in my head.

You see, I'm convinced that dreaming about exercising has almost as many health benefits as the actual exercise itself. If you don't agree, the next time you're running from that crazed maniac in your sleep, force yourself awake and then take your pulse. If my theory is correct, it'll be racing, your heart will be pounding, and you'll be so wet with sweat you'll feel like you just participated in a triathlon in Alabama in the middle of July! That's the power of the mind. It can make your body think that it's actually going through whatever it is that your mind is imagining.

It stands to reason, then, that thinking about physical exercise must do us some good, right?

All right, my doctor didn't buy it either. For some reason, he's of the opinion that my exercise program needs to take place during my waking hours to do me any good.

But doesn't he realize I could hurt myself exercising? Not only can I accidentally slap myself silly during a round of jumping jacks, but I almost broke a hip once on a treadmill when my pillow got stuck on the conveyor belt and knocked me off onto the floor.

Giving his advice the benefit of the doubt, however, I've decided to look into the possibility of getting a personal trainer to help get me in shape. So far I haven't found one I like, though. None of them will allow me to hang Krispy Kreme doughnuts off the barbells to give me an incentive for lifting weights. (If you know of one who offers this as part of his workout plan, I am taking referrals.)

Aerobics would be all right if they'd slow down the pace a little. I don't mind working out to the golden oldies, but there's a world of difference between exercising to "The Boogie Woogie Bugle Boy" and "Gentle on My Mind." I prefer the latter.

I did give tennis some thought. After all, most tennis players look like they're in pretty good shape. But tennis seems like a lot of work for nothing. All the players do is hit the ball back and forth and forth and back. How much fun could that be? And then there's all that running trying to dodge the ball. If you ask me, the only good thing about tennis is that the net comes in handy as a hammock.

That's why I maintain that brain exercises are the best. With brain exercises, you're your own personal trainer and you're in total control. In your mind you never have to wait in line to use the Nautilus equipment, you always look great in your bathing suit while swimming those laps, and there's very little risk of any physical injury. (Unless, of course, you sleepwalk. In which case I'd keep the bathtub filled with water. A high dive from the sink into an empty tub could really hurt.)

In this day of limited free time, I think brain exercising is a concept that might really catch on. And we don't have to stop with just exercising. I also have been known to have brain concerts (Celine Dion has nothing on me), give brain speeches (a standing ovation every time), and go brain skydiving (haven't landed in a tree yet), and I've even run for president in my head. (I don't know if I won yet, though. We're still counting the hanging chads.)

I get my exercise acting as a pallbearer to my friends who exercise.
CHAUNCEY DEPEW

8

Thinking Like a Tree

Have you ever heard of the Methuselah Tree? At more than forty-six hundred years old, this tree is believed to be the world's oldest living thing (except for a couple of items in the vegetable bin of my refrigerator). Because the Methuselah Tree has learned to adapt to its environment, it has survived the ages, the elements, and even mankind. It grows about an inch every hundred years. That's not a lot of growth, but it's sure and steady.

According to the Bible, Methuselah (the man after whom the tree was named) lived to be 969 years old. That's 919 years over the AARP qualification. He must have been getting some great discounts! And imagine how his friends reacted every year when they received his birthday party invitations.

"Methuselah? I thought he died."

"Says here he's turning 544. There's going to be a cookout. Think we should go?"

"Barbecue gives me indigestion."

"We oughta go. Who knows? This could be his last."

"Yeah. He is starting to slow down. Doesn't act at all like he did when he was 400."

Well, obviously, Methuselah had more birthdays. A lot more birthdays. As a matter of fact, he ended up outliving most of his family, friends, and his church's entire seniors group.

But Methuselah didn't just exist to a ripe old age, he *lived* to a ripe old age. He enjoyed his life. How do we know that? The Bible tells us that he had a son, Lamech, at the tender young age of 187, and he even went on to have other sons and daughters after that. This was a man who, at almost 200 years of age, didn't figure he was too old for Little League games or parent-teacher meetings (or whatever the equivalent to those was for that time). He didn't just sit around collecting birthday cards and counting his liver spots. He was involved in his life and in the lives of those around him. He didn't say on his one hundred eighty-seventh birthday, "How many more years could I possibly live? I'm not worth anything to anyone anymore. I think I'll just sit here and wait to die." Think about it—if he had done that, he would have thrown away 782 good years!

Now, granted, none of us are going to live to see our nine hundred sixty-ninth birthday no matter how good our vitamin pills are. People just don't live to those incredible ages anymore. Birthday candles are sold in twenty-four-packs, not one-thousand-packs. But the sad thing is most of us don't even get all that there is out of the seventy, eighty, or even ninety years that we may be allotted.

So how do we change our way of thinking about this aging process? One way is to learn from people like Methuselah, not just read about them. Obviously, Methuselah was doing something right. But what? Was he eating his oatmeal every day, working out on his treadmill, and staying away from deep-fried everything? Did he keep his stress level down by not getting involved in politics or the latest town or church gossip? Did he have a fish tank to relax in front of in an effort to lower his blood pressure? Did he keep his body fat to a perfect percentage for his size and age?

We don't know the answer to all those questions. If we did, imagine the infomercial we could make:

> Is your blood too tired to bleed? Does your skin have more of a swag than your draperies? If you answered yes, then the revolutionary Methuselah Health Malt is the drink for you! Call today and if you don't agree that the Methuselah Malt is the best health drink you've ever tasted, we'll gladly refund your money after only three requests from your attorney. So don't wait another wrinkle-forming minute! Call 1-800-SAGNSKN and place your order today! Only $19.95 for a two-week supply! Our operators are standing by. Make that call today!

As far as we know, Methuselah didn't have a miracle malt to drink or his own workout program, but he must have been doing plenty of other things right, and a good attitude had to have been at the top of the list. In the same way Methuselah the tree has had to adapt to its environment to survive through the centuries, Methuselah the man had to have done a little adapting himself.

Our attitude is important to our survival. When we become too rigid, we break. To last, we have to bend with the wind, go with Plan B if Plan A doesn't work out; in other words, we have to adapt to our circumstances.

That's how Methuselah made it.

That's how the Methuselah Tree has made it.
And that's how we'll make it, too.

> ***Change your thoughts and you
> change your world.***
> NORMAN VINCENT PEALE

9

Book Smarts

Outside of a dog, a book is a man's best friend. Inside of a dog it's too dark to read.

GROUCHO MARX

As a writer, I love books. It seems I never have enough time to read all the ones I buy, but I do enjoy collecting them. I have books stashed everywhere you can imagine—by my bed, on my desk, in the kitchen, by the bathtub—wherever I can find a spare minute to grab a paragraph or two.

I like uplifting books best. Inspirational, humorous, biographies, love stories—I love books that make me feel better after having read them (unlike the morning stock report).

My husband's favorite genre is history. His books are big and heavy and overwhelming to this one-liner mind of mine. I prefer pithy. Short and to the point. Meaningful, yet concise. Deep thoughts, but few pages (it cuts down the risk of paper cuts).

My preference for shorter books was no doubt formed in my high-school days when I'd have to carry all those heavy school books home. Even back then I preferred lighter reading. Like comic books. *Classics Illustrated* was the source for many of my research papers. They were great. Literary masterpieces such as *Oliver Twist, The Last of the Mohicans, Don Quixote,* and *Les Misérables* could all be read in one night. Maybe they weren't the real thing, but the graphics were first-rate.

My good friend Cynthia Christensen and I went to an antiquarian book fair a few years ago. It was both interesting and depressing. Antiquarian book fairs deal in old and rare books, so it was interesting to see how society has changed over the years. Old cookbooks, the original writings of people like Mark Twain and Ernest Hemingway, and old medical journals praising the benefits of leeches were all there. We spent most of the day just meandering from booth to booth, enjoying a journey through literary history. The depressing part was seeing the resale value of all the books that I had given away over the years. But who could have known those books that seemed like nothing more than dust collectors would one day be worth a small fortune? That's why Prozac sales around the country usually spike after an episode of *Appraisal Fair* has aired.

I've often wondered what it is that makes one book become a classic and another one end up on the bargain table at Barnes and Noble. A lot of different factors are involved, I'm sure.

Timeliness would surely be one. Remember how quickly Y2K books were marked down immediately after January 1, 2000? A few publishers tried to inject some life into their sales by saying the millennium bug simply had its years confused and would be striking on the "real millennium," January 1, 2001, but not many consumers bit that bait.

Usefulness, popular subject or author, and, of course, the reviews would be other reasons one book makes it and another one doesn't. Whatever it is that separates the wannabe classics from the real thing, the bottom line is there are very few worse things that can happen to a book than to be banished to the bargain table. All those dreams of it becoming a bestseller come crashing down when that 75 percent off coupon gets stuck over its title.

So whether you prefer short books or long ones, thought-provoking ones or light-reading ones, pop-up ones or picture-less ones, the important thing is to read. Books open our minds to new ideas. They take us to places we've never been before and introduce us to people we've never met. They let us have adventures we might not otherwise have. They're a twenty-dollar trip to Europe. A twelve-dollar ride in a time machine. They bring history alive and the future to our doorstep. They help us see ourselves and others through new eyes—the eyes of characters so similar to us that we think the author has been looking in our windows and taking notes. They make us laugh, cry, love, think, and face our fears. They make us better people.

Books. They're an all-you-can-eat brain buffet.

You can't tell a book by its movie.

LOUIS A. SAFIAN

10

I've Got a Ringing in My Head

*It is all right to hold a
conversation but you should
let go of it now and then.*

RICHARD ARMOUR

It seems everybody has a cell phone these days. I was in the backseat of a van once where each of the four people I was riding with was talking on their cell phones to four different parties.

On another occasion while I was waiting at an airport to board my flight, I happened to notice a man waiting at the gate across from me talking on two different cell phones. He had one pressed to his left ear and one pressed to his right ear and was conversing simultaneously with both of the callers! (It sort of gives a new meaning to the term "conference calling," doesn't it?)

At another airport, I watched a lady greet her husband with a hug, an air kiss, and a slight welcome home nod, all without missing a beat with the caller on the other end of her cell phone. Her husband seemed to be okay with it (used to it, no doubt), but it's hard to understand people like this, isn't it?

The other day while I was shopping in a department store, the lady in the next aisle over received three phone calls in a row. She didn't use her "inside" voice either. You could hear her one-sided conversation throughout the entire back third of the store. The other shoppers and I got to know so much about this woman's life that we tossed around the idea of joining her for the holidays.

I have a cell phone, but I usually don't carry it with me. The ring startles me. I realize I could attach it to my belt and set it on vibrate, but that's kind of freaky, too. I don't like being in the middle of something and suddenly getting a surprise massage.

One of the worst places to encounter a cell phone talker is at a restaurant. Why is it that people think the rest of us want to hear their minute-by-minute update on Aunt Mildred's gall bladder surgery when we're trying our best to work our way through the blue-plate special?

Driving and talking on a cell phone can be a dangerous mix. I'm sure we've all watched people swerve into the next lane, drive on the shoulder, drive over the median, run red lights, and blow stop signs all because they were talking on the telephone. Whatever happened to the good old days when people only did that on their driving tests?

Some cities are passing laws now making it illegal to talk on a cell phone and drive at the same time. That's a great idea. I've always believed people who want to talk on the phone while in a car really should have a designated driver.

But even if they pass a law in all fifty states prohibiting talking and driving, it still won't solve my problem. That's because my problem isn't talking on the telephone and driving, it's talking on the telephone and cooking. For some reason when I get lost in conversation on the telephone, I forget all about the meal I'm preparing and hardly notice the towering inferno that's in full flame on the stove behind me. But fortunately I've got conference calling, so I can call the fire department without ever losing my other party.

Alexander Graham Bell had no idea what he was starting, did he?

> **For three days after death, hair**
> **and fingernails continue to grow**
> **but phone calls taper off.**
> JOHNNY CARSON

11

Rx: Chocolate

I do not like broccoli. And I haven't liked it since I was a little kid and my mother made me eat it. And I'm President of the United States and I'm not going to eat any more broccoli.

GEORGE BUSH,
FORMER U.S. PRESIDENT

"Eat your vegetables." That's one sermon we've all heard. Our parents, doctors, nutritionists, and bathroom scales have all been preaching it to us for years, and if we're using our brains, we would follow their advice. It's good advice. Vegetables are healthy (although I think I stand with George Bush on the broccoli controversy).

We've also been told by those in the know that we should be eating seven-grain bread (which, by the way, is only one grain short of pressed board) and we need to be getting our daily supply of calcium (I'm pretty sure Milk Duds don't count).

But that's this week. The rules are always changing. One year this is bad for us. The next year it's good for us and something else is deemed unhealthy.

Take chocolate, for instance. Remember all those candy bars

you passed on, those slices of chocolate cake that you waved off at parties? Medical science has now determined that dark chocolate is rich in antioxidants and can actually help protect us against heart disease.

Excuse me? I could have been having chocolate syrup in my Metamucil all these years? Chocolate is *healthy*? Maybe even *healing*? Apparently so. But I'm not surprised. I always knew hot fudge would look great in an IV bag. Just imagine it—chocolate by prescription. Hersheys as a medical deduction on our taxes. Does life get any better than that?

This news could revolutionize the world as we know it. It means Ding Dongs can now be put on the shelf next to the ginseng. It means trick-or-treating could replace going to the gym. And it means Mary See, Sara Lee, and the Keebler elves can all be our personal trainers now.

If chocolate got a bad rap, though, doesn't it make you wonder what other food items they're unjustly keeping away from us? What else have we been told to eat in moderation when it is, in fact, good for us? What if cheesecake is actually a blood thinner? Or tiramisu an antihistamine? What if we can get all the roughage we need from brownies? What if they've been giving us wrong information all these years, making us deny ourselves unnecessarily? Have we been eating bowls of couscous and bean sprouts when all along we could have had Almond Roca? Maybe bran isn't our friend. Maybe it's nougat. Maybe oatmeal causes pimples.

Okay, maybe not. But it is interesting to think about, isn't it? . . . over a nice, healthy chocolate mocha.

Eat what you like and let the food
fight it out inside.
MARK TWAIN

12

I'll Take an 8 x 10 and Twelve Wallets

*Health nuts are going to feel
stupid someday, lying in
hospitals dying of nothing.*

REDD FOXX

While we're on the subject of health, do you know that medical science has developed a camera so small that you can swallow it and it will take pictures of your internal organs? This brings whole new possibilities to the concept of photo Christmas cards, doesn't it?

The purpose behind this ingestible camera, which they say is about the size of a large vitamin, is so people will no longer have to undergo exploratory surgery. The patient simply swallows the camera and the doctor gets a close-up view of what's going on inside.

If you ask me, this is taking the whole concept of "zooming in" a bit far. Most of us haven't had this close of a relationship with Kodak or Fuji before. We don't mind taking them along on vacations with us, but letting them hitch a ride on our breakfast is a bit intrusive, isn't it?

And just imagine all the confusion these new ingestible cameras are going to cause. From now on that gurgling noise you hear in your stomach won't mean you're hungry. It'll just mean your film's rewinding. And what happens if the flash gets stuck in the "on" position? Every time you open your mouth, it'll look like you're having a disco going on inside there.

Did they think about any of this when they invented these new cameras? I don't think so.

I also wonder how easy it is to swallow one of these things. Sure, they say it's only the size of a vitamin, but have you seen the size of some of the vitamins on the market today? It's like trying to swallow a hoagie in one bite.

Aren't you curious to know how someone came up with the idea for these ingestible cameras in the first place? Did some photography student get hungry in the lab one day and say, "Hmmm . . . this Pentax looks good. I think I'll have a bite"? Or did someone accidentally swallow their dental X ray? I realize it doesn't seem probable since dental X rays are the size of a small pillow, but maybe it happened.

I'd also like to know if anyone has determined whether or not these cameras are addictive. Sure, you might start out with the vitamin-sized camera, but after a few of those, will you find yourself craving bigger and bigger lenses? Will your addiction drive you to start hanging out in dark alleys, meeting with shadowy characters, trying to score 35-millimeters, APS cameras, Polaroids, digitals, and ultimately the mother of all cameras, the camcorder?

Where will it all stop? *Where will it all stop?*

There's the privacy issue, too. Aren't these little cameras a bit like spying on ourselves? Where's the ACLU? Shouldn't our bodies have the right to do what they're supposed to do without twenty-four-hour surveillance?

But then again . . . if our bodies are misbehaving in some life-threatening way, maybe they deserve to be caught in the act. Maybe we should get the evidence to use against them. After all, we need to make sure our organs are on the same team with us. We need to get a jump on any problems as soon as they arise.

All things considered, I suppose this new technology is a good thing. Any time we can avoid invasive surgery, we're better off. And these ingestible cameras allow us to do exactly that.

So if your doctor ever hands you a camera to swallow, just make sure it lands on your good side.

> *As for me, except for an*
> *occasional heart attack, I feel*
> *as young as I ever did.*
> ROBERT BENCHLEY

13

A Penny for Your Thoughts

If you don't value what you have, you're sure to lose it.

ABIGAIL VAN BUREN

Have you heard they're thinking about abolishing the penny? They, whoever "they" are, believe it's not all that necessary anymore. They say the Lincoln-faced coin may have lost its value. After all, if a dollar buys what a penny used to, what could a penny possibly buy? They're wondering if it's even worth the effort to continue making them anymore.

As a longtime penny supporter, I feel I must speak up, even if no one else does. Throughout my life, pennies have been my most faithful companion. No matter how little money I had in my purse at any given time, I could always find a penny. Or a handful of them. Pennies have saved me from near starvation (or at least from forgoing the fries with my burger order) on too many occasions to count. Whenever I was hungry and couldn't find any paper money in my wallet, I could always find enough pennies underneath the front seat of my car to buy something to sustain me. I didn't know how long those pennies had been living underneath the seat, hanging out with all the fuzz-covered peppermints, rusted bobby pins, wadded-up receipts, outdated coupons, and the mates to all those single socks I'd been finding in the dryer. But it didn't matter. Those pennies were still worth one cent each and when they joined forces, I was rich.

No, a penny may not be silvery or dazzling or even all that impressive monetarily, but it cheerfully does whatever it's called upon to do.

"That'll be twelve dollars and forty-two cents, please," a clerk says. And what do we do? We reach our hand into our pocket or purse and the two pennies are the first coins that report for duty.

Coincidence?

I don't think so.

A penny is also the coin of choice at most wishing wells. No one thinks twice about tossing in a penny and making a wish. If the wish comes true, they figure they got a bargain. One penny—one wish. On the other hand, if the wish doesn't come true, all they've lost is a penny. *What a deal!* But doesn't anyone think about what happens to the poor penny? One glance at the bottom of any wishing well in America will tell you a simple truth of life—pennies don't swim. They just lie there at the bottom of the well, thrust aside, drowning, and forgotten by the world.

But do they complain? No. Again, they report for duty, doing whatever is required of them.

Sometimes pennies are even abused. Each year thousands of tourists heartlessly place a penny into a pressing machine and then stand by watching as it gets flattened into some sort of sick souvenir. Often a crowd will even form to watch this cruel ritual. This isn't right, people.

I say it's high time that penny lovers start standing up for the little copper guy. We need to let people know that the penny deserves better treatment. Pennies didn't complain when we started discarding them in little bowls by the cash registers of the world, posting signs next to them that said something like "Need one? Take one. Got one? Leave one." We don't humiliate other coins like that. Why do we do it to pennies? Let's face it—when's the last time you saw a bowl full of Susan B. Anthonys sitting there just waiting for you to "take all you want"? So why the double standard?

Pennies don't complain when we ignore them after we've dropped them on the ground. Sure, we'll bend over and pick up a quarter, a dime, or even a nickel. But let a penny drop out of our hand and we pretend we've never seen it before.

"Did you drop a penny?"

"No, I didn't drop it. I think it fell out of your pocket."

"Why do you think it fell out of my pocket? It could just as easily have fallen out of your pocket."

"But it didn't. Now pick it up."

"You can't make me!"

And so the poor penny gets left there to be stepped on, rained on, and run over by semitrucks. Does it complain? Nope. Not one negative word.

Pennies are troopers. And they're worth far more than their face value. Why, do you realize if it weren't for the penny, some people (although I don't agree with the practice) wouldn't have any way of letting a waitress or waiter know they did a bad job. If it weren't for the penny, what would a bride have to put in her shoe for good luck? If it weren't for the penny, I wouldn't have gotten any advance at all on my first three books.

So you see, pennies are still used for a lot of things. And if it's true that we're known by the company we keep, then the penny is in a pretty elite group. Pennies are known to hang around an awful lot of millionaires. That's because millionaires are one group of people who have always appreciated them. If you don't believe me, just ask one about the value of the penny.

And most importantly of all, the penny is the most religious of all coins. Sure, they all say "In God We Trust," but the penny's commitment to God is a lot deeper than that. It shows up at church far more than any of the other coins.

Abolish the penny? No way.

. . . But that's just my two cents' worth.

> *If it's a penny for your thoughts*
> *and you put in your two cents*
> *worth, then someone,*
> *somewhere is*
> *making a penny.*
> STEVEN WRIGHT

14

Noises On

*Quiet minds cannot be perplexed
or frightened but go on in fortune
or misfortune at their own private
pace, like a clock during a
thunderstorm.*

ROBERT LOUIS STEVENSON

Robert Louis Stevenson was right. Quiet minds do go at their own pace in spite of what is going on around them.

We live in a noisy world. We can't stop at a red light without having some car pull up next to us with its bass blaring in our ears and making our hearts involuntarily fibrillate to the beat. We can't walk down the block without being assaulted by jackhammers tearing up the sidewalk, dogs barking, horns honking, brakes screeching, motorcycles racing by us, and car alarms going off in concert.

That's just outside. It's noisy inside, too. We've got stereos, television sets, clocks that chime, microwaves that beep, Internet connections that make that irritating *wahhhhhh-woosh* sound, telephone answering machines that bring voices into our home even when we're pretending not to be there, and even musical greeting cards.

Life is noisy!

We have smoke alarms that chirp whenever their batteries are running low, dryers that squawk when their load is done, televisions that shout their programming to us in surround sound, radios that blast the news at us, and more. We can't even wait on hold when we call a business without being forced to listen to music (usually a song we didn't like even when it was on the radio).

Our food is noisy, too. We've got cereal that snaps, crackles, and pops, along with a captain that crunches and another cereal that features cracklin' oat bran. Our sodas fizz, our steaks sizzle, and there's even a gum on the market that explodes in one's mouth (like much of my cooking).

The assault on our peace and quiet is daily and endless.

Even our bodies are noisy. We have pagers, cell phones, and wrist alarm clocks. Just today at church as the pastor was giving the invitation and the congregation was singing "We Exalt Thee," someone's cell phone started playing "Yankee Doodle Dandy." "Yankee Doodle Dandy" and "We Exalt Thee" don't make a great medley.

Elevators used to be a place where you could count on a little peace and quiet. Not anymore. Most elevators pump in old '70s and '80s tunes whether you want to revisit those decades or not. (If the FBI is looking for ways to get suspected criminals to talk, they should try stranding the suspect between floors for two hours with "Muskrat Love" blasting into his ears.)

Trash can't even keep quiet anymore. Well, trash cans anyway. Some fast food restaurants have now installed talking trash cans. Have you seen these?

I remember my first encounter with one.

"Thank you for correctly disposing of your trash," it said as I tossed in a taco wrapper.

It caught me so off guard I almost dropped my tray. I thought some environmentalist had fallen in there and couldn't get out!

I'm getting used to talking trash cans now, though. In fact, the other day one really opened up to me.

"Thank you for doing your part in keeping our world clean," it said after swallowing my chalupa wrapper and a paper cup. I then asked it how it was doing and it broke down and cried. Evidently, trash cans have issues, too.

What I'm fearing is that one of these days I'm going to come across a nagging trash can.

"Hold it, lady!" it'll say as I try to shove my trash into its mouth. *"You only took two bites of that burger! And why didn't you finish those french fries? Don't you realize there are children at other fast food restaurants who are starving with nothing to eat but dried-out chicken pieces?"*

Maybe it's just me, but it seems that there's something wrong here. While society is getting less friendly, our trash cans, ATM machines, and personal computers are getting more friendly. Our neighbor doesn't say hi, but we've got trash cans wishing us a good day. Our mail carrier doesn't even know us well enough to deliver the right mail to our home, but our PCs are bubbling over with enthusiasm to tell us, "You've got mail!"

When you think about it, it's sad, isn't it, that we have all this noise in our lives today and so little real conversation.

**Silence is the element in which
great things fashion
themselves together.**
THOMAS CARLYLE

15

Vacuum-Sealed Ideas

*Progress might have been all
right once, but it has gone
on too long.*

OGDEN NASH

I hope that one day soon the authorities will be able to catch
the guy who keeps breaking into the world's potato chip bags,
pickle jars, and milk cartons, so that the rest of us can return to
life as it used to be. It has to be some kind of hardened crimi-
nal with unparalleled strength. Why else would food companies
go to such great lengths to keep him out?

Have you ever tried opening a potato chip bag? You can try
to tear it open, pry it open, pound it open, yank it open, or
blast it open, and still you won't be able to get the bag to
release its contents. Contents, I might add, that are by now
crumbs.

Frankly, I think potato chip bag opening should be an
Olympic event. Forget weight lifting. Give those big burly ath-
letes a bag of Laura Scudder's and watch those neck veins start
to bulge!

It's not just potato chips either. Evidently, this thief has been
trying to steal our pickles, too. Some pickle jars have been

sealed so tightly nothing short of dynamite can loosen them. You try twisting, turning, tapping the jar on the floor, holding the lid over a low flame to loosen its seal, but nothing works. I've got a jar of pickles that has been in my refrigerator since 1993 because no one in the house can open it. We make attempts at regular intervals but end up just pushing it back to the rear of the refrigerator and grabbing the pork rinds instead.

I'd also like to know what kind of glue they're using on milk cartons these days. You have to tug and pull and tear at the spout, and even then you can only open it one layer at a time. You end up creating a spout that makes the milk pour in four different directions, not unlike the original udder.

Shrink-wrap beats them all, though. If you've ever tried opening a CD or a videotape that has been entombed in shrink-wrap, you know what I'm talking about. It's impossible to find the seam in shrink-wrap. You use your car keys, a pen, your teeth, but nothing seems to break through the plastic until you get out the hedge clippers. If you ask me, this is what they should be wrapping all of our toxic waste in. The deadly fumes and gases would never be able to find their way out!

The only thing worse than a shrink-wrapped product is a shrink-wrapped mind. A mind that's not only closed, it's airtight, and nothing—not an opposing opinion, not facts, not even common sense—can penetrate it. It's sealed shut!

But minds were never meant to be shrink-wrapped. And come to think of it, maybe CDs weren't either.

What we call progress is the exchange of one nuisance for another.
HAVELOCK ELLIS

16

Mind Your Business

The nice thing about egotists is that they don't talk about other people.

LUCILLE S. HARPER

Gossip may have increased over the years (thanks to talk shows, entertainment magazines, and even some after-church socials), but it's no newcomer to the scene. It's been around since early Bible days.

"Hey, Priscilla, did you hear about Balaam?"

"You mean the guy who went to visit King Balak?"

"That's the one. His wife told their neighbor, who told his sister-in-law, who told her accountant, who told his second cousin, who told me, that when Balaam returned, he claimed his donkey had been talking to him."

"Get outta town."

"I'm serious. That donkey must have the scoop on everybody!"

"A talking donkey? . . . Get outta town."

"I'm not messing with you, girlfriend. That donkey's gotta have the goods on the whole town! Just think of all he's overheard. So I'm taking him to lunch tomorrow."

"Balaam?"

"No, the donkey. But only to find out who I can 'pray' for, of course."

"Of course."

If we go farther back in time, we might overhear Noah's homeowners association meeting:

"The chair recognizes the man in the yellow striped robe."

"Thank you, Madam President. Benjamin, here. Second tent on the left in the new cul-de-sac. I wanna know when you're going to do something about that eyesore I have to look at every morning when I wake up."

"Sir, that's no way to talk about your wife."

"I'm talking about that monstrosity our neighbor Noah is building . . . although that cucumber mask of my wife's doesn't help the scenery any either. Anyway, I can't look out of my tent without seeing that ridiculous ark! It's sitting right there in the middle of his unmowed lawn . . . which is another issue I'd like to bring up."

"You're one to complain. How 'bout those three chariots that have been sitting on blocks in your yard for two years?"

"Yeah? Well, at least I'm not boarding animals without a license."

"Noah's running a pet boarding business? Here? In our subdivision? That's against the CC & Rs!"

"He's not boarding animals. He's 'boarding' animals . . . onto the ark. Yesterday I saw him loading all sorts of critters onto that thing. And I have a pretty good idea what he's up to."

"You do?"

"The ol' man's having a barbecue on his houseboat and didn't invite any of us!"

"But I thought he *had* invited us."

"He told us there was going to be a big flood, but he never mentioned a barbecue! And that, dear friends and neighbors, is precisely why we need this HOA! We simply must scrutinize the people who move into this neighborhood! Who knows what kind of riffraff are buying into our subdivision?! What do we know about this Noah, anyway?"

"We all know Noah. He's good people. Sure, this ark thing is a little weird and all, but he's still good people. And who knows . . . maybe it is going to rain like he says. The sky's looking pretty dark."

"All right, let him have his barbecue. But all I've got to say is if he thinks for one minute that he's gettin' my secret barbecue sauce recipe, he's got another think coming!"

Of course, Noah wasn't having a barbecue, and Balaam's donkey really did talk to him, but not about the other townspeople, just about what God was wanting Balaam to do. I guess it just goes to show you—gossipers don't do a lot of thinking before opening their mouths, and they can really miss the mark most of the time.

> **To avoid trouble, breathe through the nose; it keeps the mouth shut.**
> ANONYMOUS

17

Balancing Act

*People who are able to do their
own thinking should not allow
others to do it for them.*

ELBERT HUBBARD

Of all the qualities my parents possessed, I think the one I most admired in them was balance. My mother and father had their own opinions, but they weren't afraid to listen to opposing ones. They could see the points on both sides of an argument. Neither was dogmatic or had to be "right" 100 percent of the time.

Not only were my mother and father balanced individuals, they were balanced as a couple. My father was a Democrat, my mother a Republican. Neither was so blindly loyal that they wouldn't cross party lines if the better choice for the office was running on the opposing ticket. They voted for the best man. Or woman.

My parents were balanced in their faith, too. They had real faith in a real world. They didn't claim to always understand why God allowed certain trials in their lives; they simply accepted his will. They were realists. They didn't exaggerate their troubles with drama or pretend the troubles didn't exist. They understood that every life has its challenges. It was not a punishment from a judging God, neglect from an uncaring God, or a test of love from an insecure God. It was just a trial that, for whatever reason, or for no reason, they had to go through. A circumstance allowed by a God who knew his love and faithfulness would be enough to see them through it.

My parents were faithful church attenders. Beyond faithful. They went to church almost every Sunday morning, Sunday night, and Wednesday night. Notice I said *almost*. They didn't feel they had committed the unpardonable sin if, once in a while, we went on a family outing on a church night instead. Family togetherness is important to God, too. They knew that.

My parents were balanced in their careers. Especially my mother. In addition to raising five children (one with a chronic illness), she worked a full-time job, was president of the PTA, and was active on church committees, yet she never complained that she had too much to do or that someone was demanding more of her than she could give. Unlike some who volunteer out of a sense of guilt, my mother volunteered out of a sense of giving, and when you do that, there's no room, time, or reason for complaining.

It's important for us to have balance in life. To have real faith that doesn't do a disappearing act the minute life gets difficult. It's important for us to vote our conscience, even if that means crossing over our usual political lines to elect the most qualified man or woman for the job. And we need to remember that our careers and church are both important but our families are, too. God first, family second, church and career third.

Balance. Now, that's using your head.

> *Read, every day, something no one else is reading. Think, every day, something no one else is thinking. Do, every day, something no one else would be silly enough to do. It is bad for the mind to continually be part of unanimity.*
>
> CHRISTOPHER MORLEY

18
Giving Your Word

The human brain is a wonderful thing. It starts working the moment you are born, and never stops until you stand up to speak in public.

SIR GEORGE JESSEL

Words. They're one of the main ways we communicate. Words express our opinions, questions, fears, hopes, faith, frustration, and love. They convey our sadness, happiness, embarrassment, advice, desires, needs, encouragement, and ridicule. They carry our pettiness, jealousy, pride, allegiance, and more.

Words. We can do a lot with them, can't we?

Unfortunately, we can do a lot to them, as well. For instance, when did we start thinking that doubling a word would increase its emphasis?

"Was it hot?"

"Well, it wasn't hot hot. It was just hot."

Or

"Is he your boyfriend?"

"He's not my boyfriend boyfriend. He's just my boyfriend."

We manipulate their definitions, too. Remember the now

famous "That depends on what *is* is" defense used by one of our politicians?

This language manipulation is also used by some auto mechanics ("When I said I'd rotate your tires, I just meant I'd spin 'em around a few times. That'll be thirty dollars please."), real-estate salespeople ("I did too tell you the house was on an earthquake fault. See, it's right there under our Easy Relocation clause."), and even some members of the clergy ("But the offering *is* going toward keeping this ministry afloat. I have to make my yacht payment.").

Not only can we purposely change the meaning of our words, we often use them incorrectly, too. Even our national leaders. President George W. Bush himself laughs when he recalls one of his bloopers: "Rarely is the question asked: Is our children learning?" And who can forget all the great sound bites that former Vice-President Dan Quayle gave us? Among them was the famous "I believe we are on an irreversible trend toward more freedom and democracy—but that could change."

There's also Yogi Berra: "I really didn't say everything I said" and "This is like déjà vu all over again."

So you see, Democrats, Republicans, sports figures, mechanics, preachers, and just about everyone else has at some time, whether on purpose or by accident, assaulted the English language.

Sometimes instead of changing the meaning of the words and phrases, we just make them up. Take the familiar saying "in my heart of hearts." What exactly does that mean? How many hearts can we have beating inside our chest? As far as I know, it's still just one to a customer. So why do we say "heart of hearts"? We don't say, "I think I just sprained my ankle of ankles" or "He has a ruptured spleen of spleens." So why do we feel we can give ourselves additional hearts whenever we feel like it?

Even though we might misuse them, words are still important to our lives. So important that often our very first ones are documented on paper or video.

"Dada."

"Mama."

"You call this an allowance?!"

Someone's usually around to record our last words, too. Like the dying words of French grammar expert Dominique Bouhours, who is reported to have said, "I am about to—or I am going to—die: either expression is correct."

Between our exciting first ones and our philosophical last ones, most of us will utter billions of words. Big, short, one syllable, multisyllable, English, German, Spanish, French, and an assortment of other languages. We'll inform with words, inquire with words; we'll share our joys and heartaches with them, make mistakes with them, and we'll pray with them.

Words. When we think about how important they are to us, maybe we should be putting a little more thought into them.

I am a Bear of Very Little Brain, and long words Bother me.

A. A. MILNE

19

Inventive Minds

*I do not feel obliged to believe
that the same God who has
endowed us with sense, reason,
and intellect has intended
us to forgo their use.*

GALILEO GALILEI

Have you ever wondered what some inventors and designers were thinking when they came up with certain new inventions or "improved" perfectly good existing ones? Like laser-disc movies. Remember them? Those album-sized disks that were sure to revolutionize the video market? You don't hear too much about them anymore, do you? Apparently, they've gone the way of the Beta video recorder and the Edsel.

One of the first interactive computer games, created by an MIT student, was called Spacewars and could only be played on a device that required the floor space of a small house. (Imagine your kids putting one of those on their Christmas list!)

Even the zipper wasn't always a good idea. It took engineers twenty-two years to finally design a working model. For the first twenty-one years, I think they were just trying to get it unstuck!

Walter Hunt had a good invention but bad timing. He received his patent for the safety pin in 1849, but it wouldn't be until 1920 that Earle Dickson would invent the Band-Aid.

The first cameras left a lot to be desired. If you wanted to have your picture taken with one of them, you had to pose by sitting still for up to eight hours, which is proof positive that the kids pictured in all those old-time photographs couldn't possibly have had ADD.

Did you also know that the electric chair was invented by a dentist? I'm not sure how he came up with the idea, but the parallel between the two procedures is interesting to think about, isn't it?

The patent office is full of inventions still waiting to catch on with the general public. Brilliant inventions like the *dog watch*. This watch keeps dog time. I'm not kidding. I guess too many dogs were complaining about missing the mailman.

The *fork alarm* is also still awaiting its big moment in the limelight. The fork alarm is for those of us who need a little reminder to slow down and chew our food better. It comes with both a green light and a red light. As long as the green light is on, you can continue eating. But if the sensors determine that the fork is moving too quickly, the red light signals that it's time for you to slow down. If they ever make these mandatory at buffets, the forks would be lighting up so fast, it'd look like Christmas!

There are, however, plenty of brilliant inventions that more than make up for the ones that make us scratch our heads and leave us wondering why the inventors bothered applying for a patent. Inventions that have made our lives easier, our diseases less threatening, and our homes more efficient. But good or bad, marketable or not, we as a society owe these inventors a debt of gratitude. After all, when you really think about it, where would we be without the Thomas Edisons, the Benjamin Franklins, and the Alexander Graham Bells of the world? The answer is simple—in the dark, in the cold, and off the phone.

People are very open-minded
about new things—as long as
they're exactly like
the old ones.
CHARLES KETTERING

20

E-Speak

Talk is cheap because supply
exceeds demand.

AUTHOR UNKNOWN

I love e-mail. It doesn't matter whether I'm on the receiving end
or the sending end—I love it all. It's fun writing a message to
someone and getting an instant reply. Sometimes within seconds.

I also like the fact that you only have to write a few sentences. Or a few words. That's so much easier than trying to fill
a whole letter-sized piece of paper. The old-fashioned way of
writing requires at least three or four paragraphs to fill up the
page. With e-mail, all you have to do is write "Hey," and friends
will respond to you. You couldn't just write "Hey" on an 8½ x
11-inch piece of stationery. That would seem like you're snub-
bing the recipient of your musings. They probably wouldn't
even bother to write you back.

But in an e-mail, "Hey" is perfectly acceptable. In fact, it's
downright friendly.

Another terrific thing about e-mail is the fact that you can
either answer it immediately or you can take your time answering

it. Unlike a conversation, with e-mail you can give yourself a chance to think, collect your thoughts, and create that snappy comeback. In a normal conversation, you don't get that kind of time to prepare your answers. If you're slow with a comeback, like me, e-mail makes you sound much more spontaneous than you really are.

And as for all that annoying junk mail the letter carrier used to bring us every day? Well, e-mail does it, too, but at least there's a delete button.

As fun as e-mail is, though, I think some of us have taken this new form of communication to the extreme. We've allowed it to take over our communications almost to the point of being ridiculous . . . as evident from the following e-mail conversation between two cyber friends:

Date sent: Sat., March 2, 2003 8:30:12
From: FrogLegs
To: MotherGoose
Subject: Breakfast
    You up for breakfast?

Date sent: Sat., March 2, 2003 9:15:25
From: MotherGoose
To: FrogLegs
RE: Breakfast
    Sure. Where?

Date sent: Sat., March 2, 2003 11:37:45
From: FrogLegs
To: MotherGoose
RE: RE: Breakfast
    Didn't get your e-mail in time. How 'bout lunch?

Date sent: Sat., March 2, 2003 13:30:25
From: MotherGoose
To: FrogLegs

RE: RE: RE: Breakfast
> Just got the e-mail. Already ate. Let's try for dinner.

Date sent: Sat., March 2, 2003 15:12:14
From: FrogLegs
To: MotherGoose
RE: RE: RE: RE: Breakfast
> *Dinner's good. Where?*

Date sent: Sat., March 2, 2003 17:35:17
From: MotherGoose
To: FrogLegs
RE: RE: RE: RE: RE: Breakfast
> Mort's Deli. 7 P.M. See you there.

Date sent: Sat., March 2, 2003 20:13:20
From: FrogLegs
To: MotherGoose
RE: RE: RE: RE: RE: RE: Breakfast
> *Just got your message. Hope you didn't go to the deli. Sorry.*

Date sent: Sat., March 2, 2003 21:36:14
From: MotherGoose
To: FrogLegs
RE: RE: RE: RE: RE: RE: RE: Breakfast
> Waited an hour at the restaurant. Wish you had let me know.

Date sent: Sat., March 2, 2003 22:01:32
From: FrogLegs
To: MotherGoose
RE: RE: RE: RE: RE: RE: RE: RE: Breakfast
> *Didn't have my laptop with me.*

Date sent: Sat., March 2, 2003 22:43:12
From: MotherGoose
To: FrogLegs
RE: RE: RE: RE: RE: RE: RE: RE: RE: Breakfast

Understand. Maybe next time we should just use the phone. LOL (Laughing out loud).

Date sent: Sat., March 2, 2003 23:15:28
From: FrogLegs
To: MotherGoose
RE: RE: RE: RE: RE: RE: RE: RE: RE: RE: Breakfast
FOTFL (Falling on the floor laughing).

Date sent: Sat., March 2, 2003 23:45:33
From: MotherGoose
To: FrogLegs
RE: RE: RE: RE: RE: RE: RE: RE: RE: RE: RE: Breakfast
What's a phone?

Date sent: Sat., March 2, 2003 23:50:23
From: FrogLegs
To: MotherGoose
RE: RE: RE: RE: RE: RE: RE: RE: RE: RE: RE: RE: Breakfast
I think I still have one. It's a planter now. Breakfast tomorrow?

Date sent: Sat., March 2, 2003 23:55:14
From: MotherGoose
To: FrogLegs
RE: RE: RE: RE: RE: RE: RE: RE: RE: RE: RE: RE: RE: Breakfast
You got it! See you there. Oh, and e-mail me if there's a change.

I guess the bottom line is, we're communicating. And that's always a good thing, however we do it.

If confusion is the first step to knowledge, I must be a genius.

LARRY LEISSNER

21

Instant Money, Instant Headache

It is not strange . . . to mistake change for progress.

MILLARD FILLMORE

When I was growing up, we didn't have ATMs on every corner. If my parents needed cash, they either had to go to the bank, write a check at the local grocery store, or get it from "Mom's cash stash." "Mom's cash stash" was the original ATM at our house. The department store where my mother worked would cash their employees' paychecks and put the money inside small manila envelopes. My mother would then tuck that envelope away in her, well, let's just say a certain undergarment. Whenever any of us needed money, Mom would simply reach in and make a withdrawal. It was her own twenty-four-hour instant cash machine.

Contrary to today's ATMs, Mom's instant cash machine never ran out of cash. With five kids, I don't know how she did it on around a hundred dollars per week, but the money never ran out.

Today, the regular kinds of ATMs are everywhere. Besides at banks, you can find them in grocery stores, gas stations, convention centers, office buildings, and even some churches. That's not a typo. Some churches really are installing ATMs in their foyers. Evidently, pastors have found that not only does this enable their congregations to give more in the offering, but it saves the parishioners time after church so they can beat all those other denominations to the Cracker Barrel.

When ATMs first came on the scene, my husband refused to use them. He had an aversion to any machine that pretended to know him on a personal level. But if he was apprehensive then, it's gotten even worse today. ATMs used to simply refer to us as the "cardholder." Now they're our best friends. It's getting so bad, I expect to approach an ATM someday and be greeted like this on the screen:

Hello, Friend. How are you today? (Select one)

- Great. Thank you for asking.
- That depends on how much money you say I have.
- Why? Do you know something I should know?
- Just give me the cash, and no small talk. I haven't had my coffee yet.

How much money would you like me to give you? (Select one)

- How much have you got?
- Surprise me.
- A hundred bucks. I'm going to Starbucks.
- Nothing. I just needed somebody to talk to tonight.

Would you like a receipt? (Select one)

- Nah. It'll just confuse my bookkeeping.
- Not if you're going to shoot it out so fast it flies off to Idaho!
- Will you promise to use ink this time?
- No receipt. But I could use a laugh. Know any good jokes (besides my balance, that is)?

ATMs haven't gotten this personal yet, but I have a feeling they might be working on it.

Still, in spite of their intrusiveness and those screens we can barely read because of the glare, my husband did eventually break down and start using ATMs. I, on the other hand, was a fan of these convenient little cash sources as soon as they hit the market. I've had more than my share of misadventures with them, though. Like the time I accidentally pressed the Spanish language button instead of English. I was in too much of a hurry to cancel the transaction and start all over again, so figuring all those semesters of high-school Spanish couldn't have worn off entirely, I proceeded.

Unfortunately, all those semesters had worn off. After "*Hola, Amiga,*" I was lost. I had no idea what I was answering *Sí* or *No* to, so I finally cancelled the transaction and started over.

My biggest misadventure, though, happened when my son Tony and I were both waiting to use an ATM in Van Nuys, California. I had just approached the screen when we were startled by what sounded like a gunshot. We looked in the direction of the gunfire and saw a man lying on the ground. Another man, gun in hand, was crouched behind a nearby car.

My son yelled for me to duck. I yelled for him to duck. We couldn't believe what was happening, but we had to think fast.

"Get behind the building!" Tony yelled.

I did as he said while he, risking his very life, began to make his way to the car where his fiancée (now wife), Crystal, sat waiting.

All we wanted to do was get a little money out of the ATM, but now here we were in the middle of a full-blown gun battle!

We can come back later, I said to myself.

"Duck!" my son yelled again.

Peeking around the corner, I could see that Tony was now crouched and zigzagging his way toward his car, seemingly right in the line of fire.

As Tony neared the car, I noticed a policeman and another man walking toward him.

That's odd, I thought. *Why are they walking away from the scene of the crime? And why are they walking so calmly? And why isn't the policeman's gun drawn? And why are they both laughing? And why is the man who was standing in line behind us at the ATM now using the machine? Didn't he hear the gunshots? Doesn't he see that a dead man is on the ground? This is no laughing matter.*

But apparently, to them it was. I soon found out why.

"Sorry about that," the policeman said as he approached my son; then he went on to explain that they were just filming a movie.

My son and I still laugh about the incident to this day.

Our minds can take us to a lot of interesting conclusions, can't they? Tony and I truly believed we were in the middle of a robbery. There were gunshots. We could see one man was lying on the pavement. We were at a bank. Everything we were seeing was indicating that there had been a robbery.

But then again, when you consider what we paid in ATM fees, maybe there had been.

I've got all the money I'll ever need if I die by four o'clock this afternoon.
HENNY YOUNGMAN

22

A Matter of Chatter

Blessed is the man who, having nothing to say, abstains from giving us in words evidence of the fact.

GEORGE ELIOT

Have you ever experienced the "fun" of being around someone who not only thought you were entitled to their opinion but felt they had to give it to you at twice the necessary decibels? It's like they think shouting will validate their position.

Being around someone like that isn't a lot of fun, is it?

There's also the person who feels they have to monopolize the conversation; otherwise an opposing opinion might be uttered and then they'd lose their control.

People who don't take a breath between sentences or who shout their opinions at us make it difficult for the rest of us who'd like to politely get a word in edgewise. It reminds me of when I was a young child trying to board the metal carousel at the city park. I'd try to jump on, but as soon as I reached for one of the metal bars as it was approaching me, the kids who were already on the carousel would start spinning it faster and faster. My attempt to jump on usually landed me off to the side in a pile of sand.

That's what it feels like to try to talk with a conversation monopolizer. No matter how hard you try, they won't let you onto the ride.

No doubt there's a psychological reason why some people have to monopolize conversations, just as there's probably a psychological reason why we let them do it. Maybe we don't fight our way into the conversation because we want them to like us. So we let them go on and on. And on. And on. We figure if we dare to interrupt them, we'll either be risking confrontation or losing their friendship. The problem is, though, if no one ever interrupts them, they get the misconception that the entire world is hanging on their every word. The talkers continue talking, thinking they have an audience they have to please, and the listeners keep listening out of fear of having to push their way into the conversation and risk appearing confrontational. So it's a catch-22, which too often leaves the talker with a worn-out tongue and the listener with worn-out ears.

A conversation can be very stimulating when a true exchange of opinions and thought takes place. But both sides have to participate equally. That doesn't mean we have to count our words ("Hey, wait a minute, you slipped in a four-syllable word. That should count twice!"), but there does need to be an equal feeling of freedom to participate. If only one side is doing the sharing and the other side is doing nothing more than listening, it's not a conversation. It's a monologue. You can go to the theater and get that, and chances are it would be a lot more entertaining.

We learn by listening to others. By hearing what they've discovered in life and then sharing what we've discovered. There's a wealth of knowledge in the minds of men and women all across the world. If we're quiet long enough we just might hear some of it.

A good listener is not someone with nothing to say. A good listener is a good talker with a sore throat.

KATHERINE WHITEHORN

23

Fashion Non-Sense

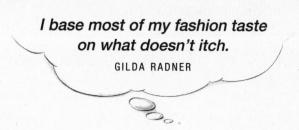

*I base most of my fashion taste
on what doesn't itch.*

GILDA RADNER

Why do we do it to ourselves? Generation after generation of women have willingly exposed themselves to the high risk of pantyhose strangulation, girdle-induced respiratory arrest, and turtleneck tracheotomies. What kind of sick people punish themselves like this?

Even men, for some unknown reason, are into some forms of fashion self-punishment. If you don't believe me, just look at the necktie. Who came up with that idea? Did some fashion designer from the Wild West watch a hanging one day and say, "Now, there's a look that could really catch on"?

Some otherwise intelligent, level-headed women have sentenced themselves to a lifetime of girdle incarceration. Every morning they insist on squeezing their bodies into those torture devices, one layer at a time. Once it's past the knees, the real tug of war begins. Up a little on the right, up a little on the left. If they're not careful, they can lose their balance and end up doing a little ballet across the room. Actually, it might be more like an opera when you consider the high notes they'll hit every time one of the metal stays pokes them in the ribs.

I've done it myself, and it leaves me asking one simple question—why? Why do we as thinking human beings do these incredibly punishing things to our bodies?

The most torturous of all has got to be pantyhose. Frankly, I can't imagine how the patent office ever approved the original application for this stuff.

"A nylon half-body suit that fits like a tourniquet but gradually loosens throughout the day until it falls in folds at the ankle like ribbon candy? And it comes in colors? Patent granted. Women'll love it!"

Spandex punishes both sexes. And in some cases, it punishes the onlooker, too. It takes a certain physique to be able to wear spandex, and many of the people we see wearing it these days have seriously violated the Spandex Rules of Engagement.

Sweats, on the other hand, are our reward for having endured decades of fashion abuse. Sweats are comfortable. Roomy. And forgiving. They keep us warm in the winter and cool in the summer. They come in a multitude of colors, and while they don't look that great with high heels and pearls, they do fit in on most occasions.

I guess the bottom line is this: Our clothes shouldn't punish us. Adam and Eve may have been acting out of guilt when they first put some on, but that was a long time ago. The debt's been paid.

*Once you can accept the
universe as matter expanding
into nothing that is something,
wearing stripes with
plaid comes easy.*

ALBERT EINSTEIN

24

Fasten Your Seat Belt

*The scientific theory I like best is
that the rings of Saturn are
composed entirely of
lost airline luggage.*

MARK RUSSELL

Even before all the new security considerations, air travel wasn't my favorite thing to do. The magazine distribution usually only makes it as far as row three. At least for the good magazines. By the time the flight attendant makes it to row forty-eight in the tail of the plane, the only choice you have is between the May 1991 issue of *Mediocre Housekeeping* and last month's issue of *Crossing Guard Life*.

I don't understand the idea behind the little curtain that separates first class from the rest of us, either. Do they really think we're going to covet their New York steak over our lunch bag? Don't they know that's precisely why we bought coach in the first place? It's so we can see what creative new thing has been done with that single slice of turkey, cheese wedge, and a cookie.

The ironic thing about all this class separation is the fact that the airlines still give coach passengers the in-flight catalog to look through. That doesn't make a lot of sense, does it? If they know we can't afford first-class tickets, how do they think we're going to buy a $100 tissue box holder? As far as I can see, the only good thing about that catalog is that it makes you think you got a deal on that $12 candy bar you bought at the airport gift shop.

Even though the items in the catalog are expensive, you have to admit they're unique. Where else can you buy things like a "turbo nose and ear hair trimmer" that comes complete with headlights and the power to whirl up to four thousand revolutions per minute? You'll never find a nasal weedwacker like this at Home Depot.

Another thing I'd like to know is why they keep the interiors of these airplanes so cold. Sure, they offer us blankets, but they're about as thick as the napkins they give us, and they don't seem very sanitary. You never know who coughed on them before you, so you're stuck in the position of having to decide between frostbite and the bubonic plague.

And I don't know about you, but I think they should let the other passengers vote on who sits in the emergency rows. How many times have you heard the announcement about the requirements for the people who sit in these rows, only to take a quick glance in their direction and find a ninety-eight-year-old couple sitting there who don't quite look up to the challenge?

"Open the what?"

"The emergency door! They want us to release the chute!"

"Cheese? I don't want any cheese. Gives me heartburn."

The airlines do seem to be giving us a little more leg room now, though. That means the blood will now be able to flow freely to at least one of our extremities. It's a start, I suppose.

Another good thing is this concept of getting bumped. No, I don't mean by the serving cart (although most of us have had that happen, too). I'm talking about getting bumped off your flight. The way I understand it is some airlines will overbook their flights. Then if everyone happens to show up, they will ask for volunteers who are willing to give up their seats. Anyone who does this will be given a seat on a later flight and awarded a travel voucher for a free trip later. As long as your travel plans are flexible, you can keep on volunteering and end up with a trip around the world—without ever taking a single flight!

All in all, I suppose airlines are doing their best to make our flight experience as enjoyable as possible under ever-changing circumstances. And when you get right down to it, that cookie in the box lunch is pretty tasty.

I haven't been everywhere, but
it's on my list.
SUSAN SONTAG

25

Jotting Down a Few Thoughts

All our words are but crumbs that fall down from the feast of the mind.

KAHLIL GIBRAN

Does anybody know what happened to the memo pad? Remember that convenient little way of communicating that we used to have? If someone wanted to leave a message for us, all they had to do was write it down on a page of the pad and leave it by the side of the phone. Or on the refrigerator. Or taped to the front door. Or on the television screen—anywhere a family member might look for a message.

Hardly anyone does that anymore. Thanks to our beepers, instant messaging on our computers, telephone answering machines with private memos, e-mail, and a host of other ways to communicate, the memo pad is no longer in vogue.

I still like the old-fashioned kind of note, though. To me, it's a lot more convenient. You don't have to turn on the computer to write it. You don't have to dial a number, then key in your own telephone number at the sound of the beep. You don't have to leave a message on a recording device before you've had a chance to gather your thoughts together and you end up leaving something incoherent on the tape. With the memo pad, you've got all the time in the world to think about what you're going to say before you write it. If you make a mistake, you simply tear off that page, toss it in the trash, and write another one. You can do this all day long if you need to. Write it. Toss it out. Write it. Toss it out.

Unless you have other means of discarding it, that is.

When I was working as a church secretary, a man who had been attending our church stopped by the office one day and asked if I would mail a tape recording of that week's sermon to a family member of his. I told him I'd be happy to take care of that for him. He then asked if he could include a note to go along with the tape. I said he could, then continued working while he prepared his note.

After writing out a few sentences, he apparently made a mistake, crossed it out, then tore off the piece of notepaper and crumpled it up. But then, instead of tossing it in the nearby trash can as I expected him to do, he ate it. (I'm pausing while you go ahead and reread that last sentence.) Now that you know it wasn't a typo, I'll proceed. I, too, thought it was a little strange, but I continued typing on the typewriter in front of me while the man wrote another note. Again, he made a mistake, crumpled up the paper, and proceeded to have seconds.

And thirds.

And fourths.

Now I was starting to feel uncomfortable. It was like *Silence of the Lambs,* only with more roughage. Luckily, a friend of mine was in another part of the church and called me about that time. Sensing the hesitation in my voice, she asked, "Is everything okay?"

"Sure, I'm not busy. Come on over," I said, slyly slipping in my message to "get over here quick!"

The man finally finished writing his note, thanked me, and left. (Apparently, he was full.) I went ahead and mailed the tape and never heard any more about it. But I've never forgotten that literary (and culinary) experience.

However we treat these little stacks of paper, I'm still a big fan of the memo pad. It's convenient, it's just the right size, and it comes in all sorts of styles and colors. And apparently, as far as entrees go, it's usually very reasonably priced.

Every man has one thing he can do better than anyone else—and usually it's reading his own handwriting.

G. NORMAN COLLIE

26

It's Gotta Be Here Somewhere

Everyone has a photographic
memory. Some don't have film.

ANONYMOUS

You can't really write a book with *think* in the title without mentioning forgetfulness. Do you realize the average person loses up to six weeks every year looking for things that he or she has misplaced at work—files, pens, computer disks, the boss.

We lose things at home, too. We misplace our glasses, car keys, slippers, remote control, checkbook, wallet, hairbrush, pens, and pencils.

When we finally find the missing item, it's often in the strangest of places. Like when we discover we put a cucumber in our purse and our cell phone in the vegetable drawer of the refrigerator.

And has this ever happened to you? You're in the middle of looking for something when you forget what it was you were looking for. Now, you would think that this would take the stress off finding the lost item. After all, if you can't remember what you lost, it stands to reason that you would no longer worry about having lost it. But that's not how it works. Forgetting what you're looking for only makes matters worse. You stress even more because you know you lost something, and the longer it takes you to find it, the more valuable you're sure it was.

When you figure we're wasting six weeks of our lives looking for articles we lose at work and at least that much time looking for things we lose at home, maybe we should try to do something about it. Maybe we could all benefit from signing up for one of those memory seminars. Haven't you wondered what goes on at them? Do they serve ginseng-spiked punch and sit around playing Pin the Tail on the Whatchamacallit?

I saw a helpful product in a catalog recently. It was an electronic locator. It came with four different pagers that would send a beeping sound to whatever item it was programmed to find. Pretty ingenious. I bought two sets. One set to use for the four items, and another set to locate the pagers for when I lose *them*.

I'm sure you've done this, too—gotten into your car, driven off, and totally forgotten that you had set something on the roof. That's always exciting, isn't it? Soda cans, your briefcase, mail, pizza. You don't realize it until you're on the freeway going seventy miles per hour and you see someone passing you waving their arms frantically. By the time you figure out that those lips being whipped in the wind are mouthing "Pizza on the roof," the pepperoni is already sliding down your windshield.

Memory loss isn't all bad, though. There are some positive things that can come out of it. If you can't remember your outstanding bills, you have a lot more spending money. If you can't recall people's names, you have a whole bunch of new friendships to make and enjoy. And if you can't remember your embarrassing moments, what's to keep you from the fun of making more?

If you can look back on your life with contentment, you have one of man's most precious gifts—a selective memory.

JIM FIEBIG

27

Borrowed Thoughts

*When I was born, I owed
twelve dollars.*

GEORGE S. KAUFMAN

Americans are in debt. I remember the days when we'd get
excited over getting a raise in our paychecks. Now we get
excited when we get a credit increase in our Visa limit.

Certainly most of the fault lies squarely with the consumer.
As consumers we need to show a lot more restraint in our
credit card purchasing. But credit card companies have to
shoulder at least some of the blame. If you're like most of us, in
any given week, you probably receive a stack of credit card
offers.

"Congratulations! You're already approved for up to $20,000!"

"Maxed out on your credit cards? Apply for another one NOW!"

*"Transfer your balance and lower your interest rate TODAY—
and keep both cards!"*

The enticements go on and on. I know a four-year-old who
routinely receives offers like these from credit card companies.
So far she hasn't accepted any, but who knows what she'll do
once she learns how to sign her name?

At first glance, these offers might seem tempting. After all, who among us couldn't use more cash? The transmission just went out on our car, our kids need braces, and there were those cute shoes that just got marked down at Macy's. But do the math. If we only make the minimum payments, we'll be paying on these purchases for the next thirty years!

It kind of takes the bargain out of the bargain, doesn't it?

My son has a pretty good philosophy. When his credit balances get too high, he puts his cards in "time out." I have a feeling a lot of the world's credit cards could use some "time out."

Credit card companies also need to show more restraint in their marketing techniques. They should do a better job of checking out whom they're sending offers of credit to (most four-year-olds don't get a big enough allowance for the monthly payments).

Companies also need to enlarge the type on their terms and stipulations and shrink the type on their hype. For "Just sign here," they use the largest lettering their computers will allow, while "If you fail to pay the minimum monthly due, we will take a limb of our choosing as collateral" is written in the tiniest script.

Have you noticed, too, how everyone is becoming a credit card company these days? In addition to banks and credit unions, our sports teams, colleges, charitable organizations, and service and professional clubs are all starting to offer their own MasterCard and Visa cards. (I once thought about issuing my own credit card to my friends and neighbors, but my paper boy already beat me to it.)

So the next time you go to use your credit card, use your head, too. While you're "making life rewarding" or enjoying that card that's "everywhere you want to be," make sure the credit card company isn't the only one that'll be having a good time in the long run.

> ***Most of today's families are
> broke. It will just take a
> depression to make
> it official.***
>
> GREGORY NUNN

28

Brain Vacations

Don't you wish there were a knob on the TV to turn up the intelligence? There's one marked "Brightness," but it doesn't work.

GALLAGHER

Have you ever gone on a brain vacation? That's what I call them. Brain vacations are different from forgetfulness. With brain vacations you haven't lost anything, forgotten anything, or misplaced anything. A brain vacation is simply voluntarily putting your brain on *pause*. You don't want to think about anything significant. You just want to sit back and veg.

There aren't any travel agencies that specialize in brain vacations, so for now it's up to us to do our own planning for these cerebral escapes. Personally, I would recommend the Television Brain Retreat. I've taken some of my most relaxing brain vacations while sitting in front of our television under the shade of our indoor Ficus tree.

Political rallies can also be a good place for a brain vacation. In fact, some political speeches actually sound like a brain vacation brochure.

"I know that's what you think I meant when I said what I didn't

mean, but this is what I meant by what I said when I said that which I didn't mean to say."

Political spin is an instant ticket to a brain vacation.

Academic or professional lectures can be a good brain vacation if the speaker talks in a monotone voice and is as exciting as a tofu sandwich.

Some motivational speakers can send your brain on a vacation, too. They're supposed to inspire you to action, but some of them don't tell you anything more than what you already know, so your brain does the only thing it can do—it retreats to regions unknown and returns just as it hears the words, "And if you buy my book, that's how you can help me become, I mean, you become a millionaire!"

Brain vacations can also be a group tour. The largest one I ever saw took place during the showing of a movie about Peter Rabbit. It was the Wednesday feature in a week of movies for kids during summer vacation. Now, there's nothing wrong with Peter Rabbit—I kind of like him actually—but this particular film had no dialogue. Not a single word. The cast was adults dressed in rabbit costumes and they bunny-hopped around the set to music. Why the theater owners thought this was a good choice for five hundred short-attention-spanned adolescents is beyond me, but when the "The End" finally scrolled across the screen and the lights came on, almost every kid in the entire theater was sound asleep. And a lot of the adults, too.

Destinations for a brain vacation are endless. So plan well and have fun. And remember, wherever you take your brain on vacation this year, make sure it's back at work before you sign any long-term contracts.

The whole art of the political speech is to put "nothing" into it. It is much more difficult than it sounds.

HILAIRE BELLOC

29

Your Credit Has Been Revoked

*I often quote myself. It adds
spice to my conversation.*
GEORGE BERNARD SHAW

When my sons were young, my husband used to take them
fishing. They would usually come home with at least a couple
of fish, but on one particular fishing excursion, they hadn't
caught anything by the time the sun was setting. That is, until
they met up with one of the biggest bass they had ever seen. He
was the length of their arms if he was an inch. He was certainly
worth all those hours they had spent out in the sun waiting for
something to take their bait. He was a beauty.

He was also dead.

I don't mean he died after they pulled him out of the water
and dropped him into their bucket. He was dead already and
was floating on his side on top of the water. The only things
missing were the breading and tartar sauce.

So they decided to bring him home. Not to eat him, of
course. After all, who knew how long he had been floating

there. But they wanted to show him off to me.

On their way back to the car, though, other fishermen saw it and couldn't help but be impressed.

"Whoa! That's a beauty! I bet he put up quite a fight!"

"Hmmmm . . . uh . . . well, uh . . ."

"Hey, let us take a picture of that baby! It's the biggest one we've seen all week!"

They all had a good laugh over the incident and never really took their "catch" seriously.

I heard of another person, though, who went a bit further with a deer. He hit it with his car, and since the deer died from the wounds, the guy had its antlers mounted. Now, I'm not a hunter (I won't even throw my leftovers in the trash for fear of hurting animals), but it seems the glory in this kind of a hunting prize is a bit tainted, isn't it? I mean, should it really count when you hit the deer with your '88 Buick? It would seem to me that the Buick has an unfair advantage over the deer. Even if the driver honked first, the deer doesn't have a sporting chance. (I understand if it's a Geo Metro that hits the deer, the deer gets to take the car home and mount it.)

And then there was a comedy writer friend of mine who once applied for a professional listing in a biographical reference book. This was one of those books that list people of notoriety. However, unlike the original *Who's Who* listings, this one should have simply been called *Who?* The book listed anyone who wanted to be listed and it rarely checked out the information to see whether or not any of it was valid. I know that because, just for fun, my friend listed outrageous credits for himself. He was, in fact, a much credited comedy writer. He was not, however, a former vice-president of the United States.

It's easy to give ourselves credit for things that we didn't really do or didn't do alone, isn't it? Maybe that's why the Academy Awards can be so refreshing. The acceptance speeches usually name people who have played a major role in the winner's life. At long last, the celebrity gets to express the praise due them.

All of us ought to do a little more of that, don't you think? To say thanks to the people to whom credit belongs. Those who have been there for us through thick and thin. Those who are the real heroes because of the endless encouragement, support, or love they have given to us. That's how we keep the circle of gratitude going, and that's also how we keep our own heads from getting too big for our necks.

> ### *Most people return small favors, acknowledge medium ones and repay greater ones—with ingratitude.*
> BENJAMIN FRANKLIN

30

Only Skin Deep

*Whatever you may look like,
marry a man your own age—as
your beauty fades, so will
his eyesight.*

PHYLLIS DILLER

I have thin hair. I admit it. And I'm okay with it. Not thrilled, but okay. I know I'm going to be one of those elderly ladies who has four hairs left on her head but insists on keeping her hair appointment every Tuesday to see what different styles her hairdresser can arrange them in. It has to be challenging for these hairstylists. Sure, they can curl the hairs to the left one week and to the right the next. The stylist can mousse them, spritz them, spray them, or just let them stand straight up in the air. She can braid three and use one as a bang. But it's still just *four* hairs.

You've got to admire these ladies, though. They're making the most of what they've got. They're not moping and complaining over the disappearance of their once thick tresses. They've graciously accepted the fact that they're down to their last four follicles and are moving on with their lives.

That's a great attitude.

Some balding men have this attitude, too. They're making the best of what they've got left. I'm sure you've seen them. They're the ones who've let their side hair grow out and are now doing the comb-over thing. It gets a little weird when it's their back hair that they've grown out and they're now combing that forward, but you've still got to admit they're doing their best to adapt to what life hands them, or in this case, takes away.

Cosmetic and hair product companies capitalize on these physical changes that happen to us. They know most of us desire to look younger, prettier, hairier, and more svelte than we really are. These companies promise us flawless, tanned, and wrinkle-free skin, six-pack abs, firm thighs, a twenty-three-inch waist, softer elbows, unbreakable nails, uncalloused feet, and enough energy to climb Mount Everest on a single granola bar.

But the simple truth is still this: real beauty comes from within. We can buy every new miracle product on the market, sign up for aerobics classes, go on all the fad diets, and spend hours in our tanning beds, but if we're not happy with who we are on the inside, we're not ever going to be happy with who we are on the outside. Thinking people know this. Hairy and tan or not.

There is a fountain of youth: it is your mind, your talents, the creativity you bring to your life and the lives of the people you love.

SOPHIA LOREN

31
A Thousand Words

*I like good strong words that
mean something.*

LOUISA MAY ALCOTT

Someone once told me that they love coming over to my house
because there are so many interesting sayings on the walls.

Besides the sign that says, "Clean Me," there are dozens of
others that feature quotes, jokes, and lots of good advice. If I
could, I'd have words all over my house.

I have a framed sign that has a Bob Hope quote. It was
given to me by fellow Bob Hope writer Gene Perret, and it says,
"I don't need writers. I only need them when I want to say
something." I also have one of Bob's cue cards with a joke of
mine from one of the television specials. It says, "I was around
when Milton Berle got his first petticoat." It was an anniversary
gift from my husband, and it's signed by Bob and all the writers.

In my kitchen there's a sign that says, "Please clean your
plate, the dog hates my cooking." There are plaques with my
own sayings, like "Rolaids—they're not just for breakfast
anymore," and "Dinner's done, call 911."

My sons had a plaque especially made for my kitchen that says, "Martha's Burn Center." It hangs on the wall next to the breakfast table.

In my dining room there's a sign that my good friend Diantha Ain gave me for Christmas last year. It says, "Live Well, Love Much, Laugh Often."

I have a sign in the guest powder room that says, "You may touch the dust, but please don't write in it."

I have a sign in the desk area where I work that says, "I can do all things through Christ who strengthens me" (Philippians 4:13 NKJV). And one in the master bedroom that says, "Be still, and know that I am God" (Psalm 46:10). There's a plaque by my front door that says, "The Lord thy God in the midst of thee is mighty, he will save, he will rejoice over thee with joy, he will rest in his love, he will joy over thee with singing" (Zephaniah 3:17 KJV).

There are words written on a clock that my son and daughter-in-law gave me for Christmas one year. It says, "God's timing is perfect."

There's a sign (I made it) in my guest room that says, "Bolton's Bed and Cereal," and one in my hallway that says, "She who laughs lasts."

I have refrigerator magnets that say an assortment of things. One has a Dan Zadra quote, "Trust your crazy ideas." Another is a Kobi Yamada quote that says, "There's no place like hope."

Another magnet features this quote by Elizabeth David: "There are people who take the heart out of you, and there are people who put it back."

Jabez's prayer is on another magnet. "Oh, that You would bless me indeed, and enlarge my territory, that Your hand would be with me, and that You would keep me from evil, that

I may not cause pain!" (1 Chronicles 4:10 NKJV).

I also have posted on the refrigerator numerous letters, e-mails, and other notes that people have given to me. I like to reread them whenever I need a lift. There's also a favorite calendar page that has a Ralph Waldo Emerson quote, "Make the most of yourself . . . for that is all there is of you."

Words. In my opinion, there's no better way to decorate your home . . . and your life.

> *The difference between the right word and the almost right word is the difference between lightning and a lightning bug.*
>
> MARK TWAIN

32

The Diner Debates

*Too bad all the people who know
how to run this country are busy
running taxicabs or cutting hair.*

GEORGE BURNS

If you're looking to find some of the smartest people on earth today, you can check the staff list at NASA or interview the world's renowned brain surgeons. Certainly, their IQs are well above average. But there is another segment of the population whose genius is all too often overlooked.

Short-order cooks.

If you don't believe me, visit a diner sometime and watch the cook handle five or six orders simultaneously all from memory. It's poetry in motion. I couldn't do that. I have a hard enough time getting my own family's order right, and I only give them two choices: "How do you want your steak? Scorched or torched?"

But short-order cooks have a lot more to memorize.

"Two eggs, sunnyside to the sky, side of grits, hash browns scattered, smothered, covered, and diced. Hotcakes, short stack, side of egg scrambled, hash browns, smothered and covered. Raisin toast, dark, hold the butter, cheese eggs, hash browns, smothered, bacon

well. Waffle and eggs, over-easy, grits, and OJ on ice."

Now close your eyes and try to repeat that from memory. It's not easy, is it?

That's why I believe short-order cooks rank right up there with some of the smartest people in history. Think about it, how long do you think Einstein would have lasted working at the grill at a Mel's Diner?

"Of course I forgot the order. I was trying to remember $E=MC^2$. Who needs this pressure? I quit!"

Short-order cooks aren't the only people who are under-appreciated for their intelligence. You'll also find some pretty smart people driving taxis. It's true. No matter where you tell some taxi drivers you need to go, they can instinctively compute the longest route to get you there. How do they do that? It's like they've memorized the entire Thomas Guide.

Taxi drivers are also gifted at calculating to the exact millimeter how close they can come to the other cars when changing lanes. Sure, you the passenger may go into cardiac arrest over all the near misses, but the taxi driver doesn't even blink. That's how confident he is of his mathematical computations. You've got to admit that's pretty impressive.

We all know about child prodigies who can play the violin or the piano or even compose incredible music, but I would like to submit that some newspaper delivery boys and girls are just as gifted. It takes someone with a substantial IQ to compute the exact force with which they have to toss the newspaper into the wind and have it land precisely at the steepest point of the roof.

So there you have it. If you ever find yourself needing a lifeline on some game show, don't automatically have the host dial up your old physics instructor or the CEO of your company.

Tell him to call your local diner. And you might want to order some hash browns to go while you're at it. Scattered, smothered, covered, and diced, of course.

> ***He's very clever, but sometimes
> his brains go to his head.***
> MARGOT ASQUITH

33

The Good Old Days?

*Children today are tyrants. They
contradict their parents, gobble
their food and tyrannize
their teachers.*

SOCRATES

The above quote wasn't said by William Bennett, President George W. Bush, Laura Bush, or any other leader of our time. It was spoken by Socrates, a philosopher who doesn't get around much on the speaking circuit these days. (I think his speaking fees are a little on the pricey side.)

Considering what he said, though, it would seem that things haven't changed a whole lot since his day. Apparently, kids were trying to push the limits even back then.

"Son, we need to talk. Your teacher said you were popping wheelies with the chariot again."

"I don't care if your school books do feel like stone tablets, Cornelius. If you've got homework to do, it's your responsibility to bring 'em home!"

"I can't wear these sandals, Mom. They're so 500 B.C."

"Get a job? No one's hiring, and there's no way I'm gonna shepherd for minimum wage!"

"Don't use that tone of voice with me, young lady! Now, I'm telling you for the last time, if that toga doesn't come to your knees, you're not wearing it!"

Sound familiar? Every generation thinks its trends, fashion sense, and attitudes are original. But if they'd do a little research, they'd discover there isn't anything new about them. That "cutting edge" look they're so proud of has simply come full circle. Fashion loves to repeat itself. This year long hair is in. Next year long hair is out. The next year it's back in again. Short skirts are in this season, out next season, and back in the following season. And bad attitudes aren't anything new either.

When we start thinking that today's youth are hopeless, it might help for us to remember Socrates. Maybe he didn't have to put up with a rock band practicing in the garage next door, but there had to have been a teenager or two on his block really getting on his nerves. Why else would he say what he said? He doesn't provide a lot of explanation along with it, but we can certainly speculate that the philosopher had his share of teenagers around who were bucking authority.

So maybe returning to the "good old days" isn't our answer after all. Maybe what we need is for each generation to teach its young people the importance of believing in and bringing out the best in themselves and others and instill in them an unshakeable faith that they will survive no matter what life brings their way. And to keep a good sense of humor about it all.

> ***Few things are more satisfying
> than seeing your own children
> have teenagers of their own.***
> DOUG LARSON

34

Listen Up!

*The fellow who thinks he knows
it all is especially annoying to
those of us who do.*

HAROLD COFFIN

Have you noticed how you can give instructions down to the very last detail, and still, people will do what they want?

Nowhere is this more evident than on airplanes. The flight attendant will announce, "Please stay in your seats with your seat belt fastened until the plane has come to a full and complete stop and the pilot has turned off the seat belt sign, indicating it is safe to move about the cabin."

But what happens? You can barely hear the end of her announcement over the simultaneous unlocking of 220 seat belts! The plane will still be rolling down the runway and passengers are getting up and doing stretching exercises in the aisle.

The reason the flight attendant makes this announcement is for our own safety. It really is, because until the plane comes to a complete stop, anything can happen.

A few years ago, a plane landing in Burbank didn't come to a stop until it reached the self-serve island at a gas station down the street. I'm not making that up. It's a true story. It was on all the news programs in Los Angeles. I guess the pilot just couldn't wait to get some nachos from the mini-mart!

Other places where some people don't listen is at banquets, theaters, churches, and other public gatherings where the emcee or announcer asks everyone to turn off their cell phones and beepers. A rather simple request, but what happens? Right in the middle of the play, the talk, the sermon, or the award presentation, a cell phone will ring and every head turns in that direction.

So where was this person during the announcement? Didn't they hear the same instructions everyone else heard?

I remember taking a test in junior high that taught each of us in our class a valuable lesson in following instructions. After the teacher distributed the test to everyone in the classroom, she told us to do exactly what the instructions said.

So we began.

The first instruction was to "read all the instructions thoroughly before proceeding." The second instruction was to write our name on the paper.

So far so good.

Then, with each step that followed, the instructions grew increasingly ridiculous. "Cross your legs." "Uncross your legs." "Put your hand on your head and pat six times." "Quack like a duck." And so on.

By the time we got to the end of the test (feeling pretty silly, I might add), we discovered that the final instruction was to do only steps one and two—read all the instructions and put our name on the test. It was very obvious which ones of us had followed the instructions completely (or had taken the test before and knew the secret).

Instructions—thinking people know it's a good idea to listen to them.

**One act of obedience is better
than one hundred sermons.**

DIETRICH BONHOEFFER

35

O Brother, Where Art Thou?

He that hath no fools, knaves, or beggars in his family was begot by a flash of lightning.

THOMAS FULLER

Relatives aren't always perfect, are they?

Look at what Jacob in the Bible had to go through with his soon-to-be father-in-law. Jacob was in love with Rachel. He promised her father that he would work for him for seven years in order to win Rachel's hand in marriage.

Jacob fulfilled his part of the bargain, but on the day of the wedding, his father-in-law tricked him by having Rachel's older sister, Leah, dress up as the bride. Talk about your funniest wedding videos. Only it wasn't so funny to Jacob. When Jacob discovered what his father-in-law, Laban, had done to him, he confronted him. Laban explained that since Leah was older, she had to get married first. Laban promised to let Jacob have Rachel, as well, but he put another price on the deal. Jacob would have to work for Laban another seven years.

"All right," Jacob said. *"I'll work another seven years, but I'd better get a discount on the tux."*

Maybe he didn't say it in those exact words, but you know he had to have been pretty upset.

Brothers don't always get along either. Look at Cain and Abel. Cain got jealous because God was more pleased with his brother's sacrifice than with his own. But he was missing the point. He didn't see that Abel had sacrificed from his firstborn stock, while he, Cain, had kept his best for himself. Cain didn't care, though. He just wanted vengeance, so he killed Abel.

The first family on earth and already they're dysfunctional.

Joseph's family was pretty dysfunctional, too. His brothers were so jealous of him that they devised a plan to kill him, as well. But then they figured out that they could make some money off of him instead, and so they sold him to a traveling caravan en route to Egypt.

Not exactly *Little House on the Prairie*, is it?

But as mean, self-serving, and unloving as some families can be, there are also those who love tirelessly. Take Ruth and Naomi. After Naomi's husband and sons died, she decided she needed to relocate. She told her daughters-in-law to return to their own mothers and she would be going to live in her homeland. But Ruth loved Naomi so much that she refused to leave. Even after Naomi's other daughter-in-law left, Ruth went with Naomi and they became one of the most successful mother-in-law stories on record today.

See, it can happen.

Joseph's brothers ultimately ended up finding that kind of love in their family, too.

After arriving in Egypt, and through a series of remarkable events, Joseph was made second in command over all the land,

and when a great famine hit, Joseph was instrumental in saving his brothers' lives. Did they deserve it? Of course not. Was Joseph in denial of how they had treated him and was he acting out of weakness? No. In fact, Joseph addressed their abuse head on: "You intended to harm me, but God intended it for good . . ." (Genesis 50:20).

Families—big, little, rich, poor, indifferent, judgmental, forgiving, grudge-carrying, loving, or bickering—they do keep life interesting, don't they?

> *Like all the best families, we have our share of eccentricities, of impetuous and wayward youngsters and of family disagreements.*
>
> QUEEN ELIZABETH II

36

When You Care Enough

Father's Day is like Mother's Day
except the gift is cheaper.
ANONYMOUS

Have you noticed how greeting cards are getting more and more specific? There are birthday cards for mothers, fathers, brothers, sisters, sons, daughters, grandparents, uncles, aunts, grandchildren, great-grandchildren, in-laws, pastors, teachers, pets, and just about everyone else you can think of.

Aside from the person-specific cards, there are situation-specific cards, too. There are cards for the ill, the hospitalized, the injured, friends you love, friends you've offended, and friends you'd like to get to know better.

There are cards for life transitions, such as moving away, retiring, promotion, job transfer, achievements, disappoint-ments, marriage, anniversary, divorce, birth, sorrow, and gradu-ation.

Holiday cards include sentiments for a happy New Year, Valentine's Day, St. Patrick's Day, Mother's Day, Father's Day, the

Fourth of July, Thanksgiving, Christmas, and even Groundhog Day.

With all the cards on the market today, one might think that every possible situation and occasion in life has already been covered. One might think that, but one would be wrong. I've found a few that Hallmark, American Greetings, and all the other card companies have missed. Maybe I'm wrong, but so far I haven't seen a hypochondriac line of greeting cards. The cards could say things like . . .

> *Sorry to hear about your illness.*
> *Again. And again. And again.*
> Or . . .
> *Heard you were in the hospital. Congratulations! We knew you could do it!*
> Or . . .
> *Wishing you a lengthy recovery and many more years of wonderful symptoms.*

I also believe the market is wide open for birthday greetings for those people who have never been nice to you, but because of various circumstances, you still feel the need to acknowledge their birthday. But all those cards that say "Happy birthday to a wonderful guy" or "Wishing a sweet gal a happy birthday" just don't quite do it, do they?

Where are the cards that say, *Of course you deserve a regal birthday! What else do you give someone who's been a royal pain in the neck?!*

I'm not sure, but I think there could be a market for cards like these. So far Hallmark hasn't called. But I figure it'll be any day now.

*The real art of conversation is
not only to say the right thing at
the right place but to leave
unsaid the wrong thing at the
tempting moment.*

DOROTHY NEVILL

37

Guilty Pleas

*Mothers, food, love, and career,
the four major guilt groups.*

CATHY GUISEWITE

Remember in school when you had to write an essay on where you went on your summer vacation? You wrote about your trip to the Grand Canyon, Yosemite, or Washington, D.C., your visit to your grandparents' farm or to some other wonderful place.

I'm pretty sure none of us wrote about the trip we take most often in life—The Guilt Trip.

With guilt trips you don't need airfare, a rental car, or even a hotel reservation. All you need is your mind. And forget the two-bag limit. On a guilt trip, you can take along as much baggage as you like. In fact, the more baggage the merrier.

You don't need a travel agent to book a guilt trip either. Anyone can book it for you.

Friends can send you on one:

"Remember the time I let you have the cherry off my sundae when we were in the fifth grade? Well, I sure remember, so co-sign this loan for me."

Parents can book some of the most scenic guilt trips.

"One of these days I'm not going to be around. You're going to pick up the phone, wanting to hear my voice, but I'm not going to be there."

"You're healthier than me, Mom."

"I'm not talking about dying. I'm talking about moving and not hooking up call forwarding!"

Another popular guilt trip destination is Labor Island.

"Twenty-three hours of labor! Not twenty. Not fifteen. Twenty-three hours! Do you have any idea how loooooooooong twenty-three hours of labor is? No, of course you don't because you sneezed and had your children. But I had you the hard way. No anesthesia, no La Maize classes, just me and the pain. The whole town still talks about the screams. I go through that kind of pain for you and you can't pick up the phone and call?"

Dieters can send us on a guilt trip if we dare to enjoy our food while *they're* on their diet.

"You're not going to eat all those french fries, are you?"

"I was thinking about it."

"Do you have any idea how much cholesterol is in a single cup of french fries?"

"Not offhand, no."

"Enough to clog a Slurpee straw. So let me have half of them. It'll be healthier for you. And speaking of Slurpees, you gonna drink all that one yourself or are you going to share?"

Some Christians can also be travel agents for guilt trips.

"I see you came in late to church today. If I was that late, I wouldn't have even bothered coming."

Or

"I realize you're already serving on the visitation committee, the youth board, the Sunday school council, and choir, but children's

church really needs someone like you, and if you were really listening to God's voice . . ."

Life's too short for guilt trips. So the next time you book a guilt trip, or someone else books it for you, cancel it immediately. Guilt trips make for lousy vacation pictures.

Guilt: the gift that keeps on giving.
ERMA BOMBECK

38

Weight Lifting

*If thine enemy offend thee,
give his child a drum.*

ANCIENT CHINESE PROVERB

Some of us spend far too much time thinking about things that happened in the past. I knew a lady once who got so mad at a family member that she cut her out of all the family pictures. Looking through her family album was like looking over a collection of doilies. No matter how many people were in the picture, there was always one head missing.

Nowadays, there are photo centers where you can take your family pictures and digitally crop anyone you want out of the photo. Grudge carrying has gone high tech. The picture ends up looking almost as good as the original, and for those who enjoy carrying a grudge this far, it's much better than having family photos with big gaping holes in the middle of them.

But this lady didn't live long enough to see this advancement in photographic technology. She was forced to carry out her grudges the old-fashioned way.

The remarkable thing about this particular grudge was how old it was. The woman was close to eighty years old and the incident happened with her family member when they were teenagers! If only our memories of the good things that happen to us in life were as well preserved.

This woman didn't just hold a grudge against this family member, though. She had a whole list of offenders, and she was emphatic with her instructions of not wanting a single one of these people invited to her funeral. Throughout her lifetime, she continued adding names to her "Don't Invite to My Funeral" list until the Don't Invite list was longer than the Invite list.

Grudges can get pretty ridiculous if we let them, can't they?

The way I see it, there are only ten good reasons to allow your mind and heart to carry a grudge:

1. If you want to reward the person who hurt you by keeping you absorbed in the situation while they go on with their life.
2. If you want to keep your mind off all those other bothersome things, like the people in your life who truly love you and who've never hurt you.
3. If you want all that wallowing in self-pity to keep wonderful new friends away so you'll never have to risk getting hurt again.
4. If you want to give gossipers more fuel to talk about over lunch.
5. If you want to give yourself a sour expression, which can lead to major wrinkles.
6. If you want to make the person who hurt you feel triumphant because they've successfully hijacked your joy.
7. If you want to prevent yourself from achieving what you were meant to achieve in life.
8. If you want to wear yourself out so you won't have the energy for all those other exhausting things like

parties, picnics, strolls in the park, road trips, and vacations with loved ones.

9. If you want to react to your pain by eating a diet of junk food and clogging your arteries.

10. If you enjoy tossing and turning at night and getting those lovely bags under your eyes.

Still feel like carrying that grudge?

Probably not.

My mother used to carry a purse that would have strained the back of any body builder. She kept everything in there—her wallet, makeup, bills, old receipts, catalogs, junk mail, phone books, ledger books. You name it, Mom had it in her purse. Her purses were her filing cabinets. Whenever she got a new purse, she'd just pack the old one away, papers and all, then start all over again. She had her 1979 purse, her 1980 purse, and so on.

After my mother was diagnosed with lymphoma and the disease began taking a toll on her strength, I managed to convince her to start leaving her purse at home and just carry her wallet. At first she felt a bit naked without that suitcase of a purse, but after a while she loved the freedom. She had been carrying all that unnecessary weight for years, a load she just accepted as her responsibility to carry. Once she gave herself permission to let it go and leave that baggage behind, there was a remarkable change that took place. The change didn't take place in the purse. It was in her face. The purse hadn't changed. It still weighed the same as it always did. Its contents remained the same. The only difference was she wasn't carrying it with her anymore.

If there's someone in your life who has hurt you, either recently or decades ago, that pain is real. Maybe you honestly didn't deserve it. Maybe you're 100 percent right. But you can choose to fill your mind with that situation morning, noon, and night, or you can let it go. When you choose to do the latter, to set that pain aside and not carry it anymore, you're not changing the facts of that hurt. True forgiveness is seeing the hurt, recognizing the hurt, but willingly forfeiting your right to revenge. It's clearing your mind to think about other things.

Life's too short to carry heavy purses.

> *To carry a grudge is like being*
> *stung to death by one bee.*
> WILLIAM H. WALTON

39

A Mind at Peace

*Worry often gives a small
thing a big shadow.*
SWEDISH PROVERB

Worry. Over the years we've worried about a lot of things, haven't we? We've worried about comets crashing to the earth and meteors falling on us. We've worried about the Y2K bug causing widespread havoc, massive riots, food shortages, and a worldwide disrupted banking system. We've worried about a major earthquake separating California from the mainland and sending it floating away like a giant bodyboard.

We've worried about it all.

Some of us did more than worry. We headed for the hills. Or bunkers. We bought generators, gas masks, and real estate in inland California with the hope of it becoming beachfront property someday. We stocked up on food, water, guns, and everything else we could get our hands on.

But what did all that worry gain us? Ulcers. Furrowed brows. Sleepless nights. And a cellar full of canned beets.

The comets came and went, and the earth kept on spinning. Some meteors fell (as they have done for thousands of years), but none of them landed on our coffee tables. Y2K came and went without so much as a blip on our computer screens, leaving some of us standing there with a lot of powdered egg on our faces. And even though California has certainly had its share of earthquakes, none have been big enough to send the Golden State floating off to Hawaii.

So why did we worry?

Because we enjoy it. We must. Why else would we get caught up in all these panic-driven scenarios? Whatever the fear of the moment is, it will be covered by all the major news outlets. It'll be the topic of our conversation at work, in our homes, and at church. It'll be the only thing people are talking about until it passes and the next scare comes along.

The human mind is powerful. What we imagine happening can adversely affect our bodies almost as much as if it actually happened. In fact, sometimes it can do even more damage because in a real crisis, human nature seems to rise to the occasion, performing amazing acts of bravery. In an imagined crisis, the strength isn't there, only the worry and stress.

The Bible tells us that we're not to borrow trouble from tomorrow. Each day is going to come with its own set of problems. If we spend today worrying about tomorrow's problems, or if we're still fretting over yesterday's problems, then we won't have any stamina to handle what we're going to be called upon today to handle. We need to take each day, and its challenges, as it comes.

So the next time it looks like a meteor is headed your way, wear a hard hat if you must, but don't lie awake at night worrying over it. There's not a thing you can do about it, and besides, just think of how much money you're going to save on that in-ground swimming pool you've always wanted.

Don't worry about the world coming to an end today. It is already tomorrow in Australia.

CHARLES SCHULZ

40

I've Got a Bone to Pick With My Clone

A human being is a single being.
Unique and unrepeatable.

EILEEN CADDY

I've come to the conclusion that each one of us has a twin walking around in another part of the world. Whenever I travel, I'm amazed at how many friends I "almost" see. That waitress in Houston looks just like the keyboardist at our church. That taxi driver in Washington, D.C., is the near perfect image of our men's group leader. And the five-year-old boy sitting next to me on the airplane (and I use the term "sitting" loosely) looks remarkably like our neighbor's kid. It makes you wonder if they've been cloning us for years and *60 Minutes* just hasn't aired the exposé yet.

Frankly, I don't know what I'd do if I ever ran into myself in another part of the world. Talk about your awkward moments. What would I say?

"Hi, how am I?"

"Fine, thanks, and me?"

Would I try to avoid myself, not wanting to get stuck in a conversation that I know I wouldn't be interested in? After all, if it's my clone, I'd already know everything I have to say so what fun is that? I'd know the punch line to every joke and the end to every story. I would have heard all my opinions a hundred times before, and if I complimented my new hairstyle, I'd know I would be saying that just to make me feel better. I couldn't compliment my new shoes because I'd know they were killing my feet. I wouldn't accept an invitation from myself for lunch either, because who'd pick up the check? Me or me? Either way I'd be stuck with it.

I don't know why we'd want to venture into the unknown world of cloning anyway. Aren't there enough people standing in line in front of us at the DMV already? Our freeways are overcrowded, our cities are overcrowded, our schools are over-crowded, and now someone wants to double the population? Even aside from the moral issues of cloning, there just isn't room for a duplicate of each of us.

But the biggest argument against cloning is a financial one. Businesses would never be able to give away that many group discounts.

> *You've gotta be original, because*
> *if you're like someone else, what*
> *do they need you for?*
> BERNADETTE PETERS

41

Are You Having Fun Yet?

Nobody really cares if you're miserable, so you might as well be happy.

CYNTHIA NELMS

I'm amazed at the number of people walking this earth who enjoy being miserable. No matter what you suggest, they have a reason they can't do it.

"Wanna go for a drive?"

"Can't. I get carsick."

Or

"You've just won a free vacation!"

"Thanks, but I've got too much work to do."

Or

"Let's go to Disneyland!"

"I would, but I'm allergic to mice."

Whatever you suggest that comes close to resembling a good time, they've got a reason why they can't participate. They sabotage their own fun with their negativity and excuses.

Down deep, I believe most people want to have a good time during their journey through life. No one came into this world with the attitude, "All right, let's get this over with." No, they entered this new life full of awe, excitement, and lots and lots of potential. And they came equipped with a natural ability to smile and laugh.

Somewhere along the way, though, some of us changed our minds and decided to take life way too seriously. We became afraid to use the laugh muscles that came with the original packaging. Instead of using this natural God-given pressure valve, we've allowed our smiles to sag and our negative outlook to drag us down.

Life wasn't meant to be lived this way. God intended each new dawning to be met with anticipation, not apprehension; wonder, not whining.

But every day the news is filled with depressing stories that bring us down. We have to deal with rude and negative people. So how in the world do we keep our joy?

The Bible gives us the secret in Philippians 4:8. It says for us to find whatever is true, whatever is honest, whatever is just, whatever is pure, whatever is lovely, whatever is of good report, whatever is virtuous and worthy of praise, and then we should think on these things. In other words, wherever we let our mind go, our attitude is sure to follow. If we allow our thoughts to feed on all the garbage of life, then that's where it's going to stay. In the dumps. But if we find the positive things in life and fill our mind with those thoughts, our outlook is going to be positive. What goes in is what comes out. So if you'd like to feel a little more joy throughout your day, try being more selective with what you're letting into your mind. The world offers a daily smorgasbord of both good and bad to choose from. What you scoop up onto your plate is your choice.

> **The best blush to use is laughter:**
> **It puts roses in your cheeks**
> **and in your soul.**
> LINDA KNIGHT

42

Brain Bloopers

When you are a Bear of Very Little Brain, and you Think of Things, you find sometimes that a Thing which seemed very Thingish inside you is quite different when it gets out into the open and has other people looking at it.

A. A. MILNE

Have you ever made a stupid mistake? Of course you have. We all have. We mean to say one thing, but something entirely different comes out of our mouths. We spend five minutes pushing on a door that has a sign hanging on it that clearly says *Pull*. We shriek with excitement over seeing that long lost friend at the mall only to find out it's not her.

Why? Because we're fallible.

Here's an e-mail that I sent to a good friend of mine who had just given me a new photo/credit card holder. Eager to fill the holder with photos, this is what I wrote to her:

"Linda . . . Mary and Don sent me a picture of themselves, and now I need one from you and Iradg. If you've got a wallet, please send it. Martha"

I knew that I was requesting a wallet-sized picture of her and her husband, not her actual wallet. But that's not how the e-mail read.

Linda, in good humor, wrote back.

"I've got a wallet, but I plan to keep it."

Another e-mail misunderstanding happened with Torry Martin, a comedian friend of mine whom I had been helping out with his act. He was writing to say that he appreciated some writing I had been doing for him, but then he added, *"If I end up getting booked at a few places, that means I'll be bringing in some money and I would like to be able to start paying you for all you do, but I need to know what you charge for the kind of help you give me. It's not enough for me to simply appreciate all your help. You need to be constipated, too."*

I had a good laugh over the typo and knew what he meant to say . . . I think.

An introduction that I had written for a Bob Hope television special was later featured on one of his blooper shows. It was an introduction for Garth Brooks. I had written, "Garth Brooks is one of the most sought after performers in show business today." But Bob kept getting tongue-tied and said, "Garth Brooks is one of the most sawed off performers in show business today."

We can do all the right things. We can think before we talk. Think before we write. Think before we act. Yet we'll still make mistakes. Why? We're human, and humans are fallible.

So how should we act knowing that there's a very real possibility that we're going to fail? The same way we'd act knowing there's a very real possibility that we could succeed.

I think perfectionism is based on the obsessive belief that if you run carefully enough, hitting each stepping-stone just right, you won't have to die. The truth is that you will die anyway and that a lot of people who aren't even looking at their feet are going to do a whole lot better than you, and have a lot more fun while they're doing it.

ANNE LAMOTT

43

Look Before You Jump
(to Conclusions)

A mountain in labour shouted so loud that everyone, summoned by the noise, ran up expecting that she would be delivered of a city bigger than Paris; she brought forth a mouse.

JEAN DE LA FONTAINE

Last night I was up wrapping Christmas presents until around two o'clock in the morning. It's August. I'm a bit early, I know, but I love Christmas.

After finishing the last gift, I walked into the kitchen to get a drink of water. I didn't bother turning on the kitchen light because the light from the hallway was shining in there just enough so I could see where I was walking.

I got the water and turned to leave, but as I did, I was startled by a deep, husky voice coming from the far, dark corner of the room.

"What are you lookin' at?!" it demanded.

I almost dropped my glass!

Think . . . think . . . I kept telling myself. *Do something! Run! Hit him over the head with a burnt dinner roll! Something!*

But all I could do was stand there. I couldn't even manage a scream.

"*What are you lookin' at?*" the voice repeated with the exact same volume and inflections. Only now the voice sounded slightly familiar. I couldn't put my finger on who it was, but I knew I'd heard that voice before. I was certain it wasn't any member of my family, but still, there was that hint of familiarity about it. *Who is it and what is he doing in our kitchen at two o'clock in the morning?*

Just then the voice bellowed through the darkness again.

"*Haven't you ever seen a talking fish before?*"

A talking fish?!

Okay. Mystery solved. It was the fish on a plaque that our son had given his dad a few years ago. You know, the fish that says eight or ten different sarcastic phrases when you walk by it. For some reason, though, on this particular night it just came on all by itself, even though I was all the way on the other side of the room.

I had a good laugh at myself because for a few seconds there I truly thought I was in danger. In reality, I wasn't in any danger at all. (Although after the scare it gave me, that fish was in danger of getting filleted.)

If we're not careful, our minds can fill in a lot of blanks incorrectly, can't they? We can think this about that or that about this when this has nothing to do with that and that doesn't resemble this in the least. Our minds convince us of one thing when something completely different is true. Jumping to conclusions, when they're the wrong conclusions, can jeopardize relationships, our jobs, and our peace of mind.

I do a lot of traveling with my work. When you write comedy, it's best to be a moving target. Traveling, though, involves staying in hotels, and that can be challenging because you never know if the people in the room next to you are as intent on getting a good night's sleep as you are.

On one such trip, I was exhausted by the time I checked into my room and was therefore looking forward to a little peace and quiet. Unfortunately, the people in the adjoining room weren't. I could hear the muffled voices from their television set coming through the wall just behind the head of my bed. The voices weren't blaring, but just loud enough to keep me awake. I thought about calling the desk clerk, but since it was almost midnight, I decided to wait, figuring it would be just a matter of time before they turned it off.

One o'clock came and the noise continued. Then two o'clock. And three o'clock. Finally, by four in the morning, my patience had finally worn out. I don't like causing problems, but this was getting a little ridiculous. I had been long-suffering long enough. Besides, what if something had happened to the person in the next room and they couldn't turn off the television set?

As I reached for the phone to dial the operator, I noticed a little flashing red light on the clock radio by my bed. That's odd, I thought. I looked at the light and listened again to the voices in the next room. It soon became all too clear that those muffled sounds weren't coming from the television next door but from the clock radio in my own room!

Jumping to conclusions may be exercise, but instead of losing weight, all we'll ever lose is sleep.

The difference between fiction and reality? Fiction has to make sense.
TOM CLANCY

44

I Think, Therefore I Laugh

Humor helps us to think out of the box. The average child laughs about four hundred times per day, the average adult laughs only fifteen times per day. What happened to the other 385 laughs?

ANONYMOUS

Did you know the human body is designed to handle an unlimited number of laughs? None of us were born with a warning, "Do not exceed recommended dosage of laughter in a twenty-four-hour period," tattooed on our forehead. From birth to the moment of our death, we are free to enjoy as much laughter as we want. In fact, look at the longevity of some of the greatest comics of our time: George Burns lived to be 100 years old. Milton Berle was 93 when he passed away, and Lucille Ball was 77. Red Skelton was 84, and Bob Hope's one-hundredth birthday was in May of 2003.

Obviously, a good sense of humor is healthy.

Exercise is healthy, but only to a point. We can sweat to just so many oldies. We can run a limited number of miles before we end up collapsing on the jogging trail. We can only do so many push-ups, sit-ups, or knee-bends before our muscles give out and go on strike. Exercise is good for us, but in moderation.

We can't eat all the red meat we want either. Or butter. Or sugar. Our bodies weren't built to handle an overabundance of any of these products. We can certainly handle some, but we shouldn't pour that five-pound bag of C & H onto our Shredded Wheat.

But laughter? As far as our vital organs are concerned, there's no limit. Our heart won't start beating irregularly if we have a fit of laughter. We won't dehydrate, our kidneys won't start shutting down, and we won't run the risk of our lungs collapsing during a giggle fest. In fact, the more laughter we have in our lives, the healthier we could become. Laughter is good for us.

It's been said that a hearty laugh burns calories. Laughter is also believed to release endorphins into our system that can change our outlook on life and help prevent depression.

Laughter can have positive effects on our immune system, too. It can even improve our social life, because people are far more attracted to those who laugh than those who whine.

Not only can we laugh as much as we want, we can laugh whenever we want. Laughter isn't seasonal. We can do it in the spring, summer, fall, and winter. Laughter doesn't have a curfew. We can stay up and laugh as late as we want. And we can do it first thing in the morning.

We don't have to worry about laughter putting us in debt

either. Laughter's free. Unlike that trip to an amusement park, buying a new car, or going outlet shopping, laughter won't stretch our already stretched-out budget. We can enjoy as much laughter as we want and we'll never go over our credit line or be forced to pay 20 percent interest.

It's perfectly legal to laugh and drive, too. (Although if you're in the car by yourself, people might start to stare.)

And laughter doesn't have an expiration date. No matter how old you are, your sense of humor can be just as good as it was when you were a child. It may need a little dusting off, but it isn't due to expire until you do.

So go on, laugh it up. Give your mind a break from the stresses of life. Laughter will never give you a headache. But it can certainly help heal the one you might already have.

**If you lose the power to laugh,
you lose the power to think.**
CLARENCE DARROW

45

The Thinkers' Bill of Rights

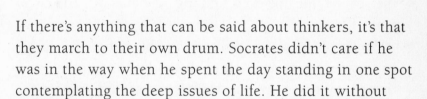

Be who you are and say what you feel, because those who mind don't matter and those who matter don't mind.

DR. SEUSS

If there's anything that can be said about thinkers, it's that they march to their own drum. Socrates didn't care if he was in the way when he spent the day standing in one spot contemplating the deep issues of life. He did it without apology.

Thinkers don't worry about what other people might say. They know their thinking is important work. It might change the whole world. Or at the very least their world. They give themselves permission to think because they know they have to do it to live. Thinkers are driven. They're committed. But the world doesn't always afford them their thinking space. That's why I believe thinkers need their own Bill of Rights.

Thinkers' Bill of Rights

- A thinker shall have the right to drive his or her car in the fast lane of the freeway with the left turn signal blinking.
- A thinker shall have the right to stare at the vegetables in the grocery store for prolonged periods of time without disturbance. Talking to them, however, could be disconcerting to the other shoppers and therefore should only be done when absolutely necessary.
- A thinker shall have the right to voice his or her opinion at the television set and to do it at whatever volume deemed necessary. (The tossing of objects at the television, however, could be hazardous and should be reserved for political speeches, editorialized news reporting, or nights when the *Everybody Loves Raymond* reruns get preempted.)
- A thinker shall have the right to sleep late. Scientists have proven (or are surely on the verge of proving) that some of the deepest thinking occurs during the hours of 11 A.M. and noon.
- A thinker shall have the right to close his or her eyes during two-hour-long sermons. He or she is obviously lost in thought over deep spiritual matters and should not be disturbed (unless the snoring gets disruptive).
- A thinker shall have the right to ponder the greenness of the *go* light for a minimum of five seconds before venturing out into the intersection.
- A thinker shall have the right to stare at his or her own belly button for as long as it takes to come up with the answers to life's most difficult questions.
- A thinker shall have the right to a steady supply of brain food (or Krispy Kreme doughnuts).

- A thinker shall have the right to engage in daily debates with non-thinkers but may opt out if the debate ever gets too boring or the box of Krispy Kreme doughnuts is threatened in any way.
- A thinker shall have the right to stand and defend his or her right to think. Or to go home and sleep on it, whichever seems more inviting at the time.

> ### *I not only use all the brains that I have, but all that I can borrow.*
> WOODROW WILSON